Why Forgiveness Makes Sense

Heal your heart,
rebuild your life

Gregory Kirby

Copyright © 2007 Gregory Kirby

Printed and bound in the United States of America. All rights reserved. No part of this book may be reproduced in any form or by any means without prior written consent of the publisher, except for in brief quotes used in reviews. For information, contact G K Ministries, 7016 Steeple Chase Plaza, Shreveport, LA 71129.

**Publisher's Cataloging-in-Publication
(Provided by Quality Books, Inc.)**

Kirby, Gregory.
  Why forgiveness makes sense : Heal your heart, rebuild your life/by Gregory Kirby.
  p. cm.
  LCCN 2007920442
  ISBN-13: 978-0-9792653-0-3
  ISBN-10: 0-9792653-0-4

  1. Forgiveness—Psychology. 2. Forgiveness—Religious aspects—Christianity. I. Title.

BF637.F67K57 2007   158.2
                        QBI07-600030

Foreword

Too often, instead of experiencing the joy of the Lord, Christians are plagued by discouragement and doubt. Why? The answer is simple, yet profound. The answer lies in our understanding of who we are in Christ, and what it means to forgive and be forgiven. When we are uncertain of our relationship with God, "wondering day after day if he has truly forgiven us," then we cannot be certain of our relationships with each other. Living on edge like that produces anger, resentment, a lack of confidence, and other negative emotions. But there is a way out of that place.

Why Forgiveness Makes Sense will help you discover and implement God's power in your life. In its pages, you will discover a spiritual adventure that will take you from bondage to freedom and joy in Christ. This book will help you move beyond just talking about the joy you experience through Jesus Christ to actually gaining a new perspective as you understand the deep significance of forgiveness in your life. You will learn why forgiveness is a must, how to seek it, how to grant it, and how to know if you've received it. Once you unlock the keys to forgiveness, your whole spiritual experience will change.

You will live each day with a new view of your life and your place in this world. Gain confidence to tackle the challenges you've been facing. Read this book and let forgiveness create unspeakable joy in your heart.

J. Rascoe Gant, Jr., D. Min.
Calvary Missionary Baptist Church
Shreveport, Louisiana

Foreword

Pastor Gregory Kirby is blessed with the awesome knack of making it plain and practical. I immediately related to the anger, resentment, guilt, and bitterness associated with an unforgiving spirit. Excuse me for living, but I have forgiveness issues and must constantly pray and practice doing better. The book is a revelation.

Pastor Kirby has provided an eloquent and simplistic ground-floor discussion of why forgiveness makes sense and more significantly, he chose to deal with how to make it happen. The resolve to let go and let God may come easily. But the process to that end is perplexing; forgiving others, forgiving ourselves, reconciling, trusting, and rebuilding are all tough.

The Robert Newsome testimony, Pastor Kirby's personal encounters, the marriages, the families, business partner ventures and the Amish community ordeal provide brutal real-life situational challenges that appear to be justifications for grudging and hating. In each case, Pastor Kirby reminds and explains that if God settles the score, he will work it for good. The book is speckled with Biblical references that offer support, models of Christian behaviors and affirmations that without God, we can do nothing.

Thank God for a personal kinship with Pastor Kirby and his church family. Truly, I am richer for having them in my life. It is my esteemed pleasure to commend him on the completion of his second book, *Why Forgiveness Makes Sense*, and to recommend it to you as a must-have resource to heal your heart and rebuild your life.

I wish you peace that passeth all understanding.

Mary Nash Robinson, Ph.D.
Assistant Superintendent, Human Resources
Caddo Public Schools
Shreveport, Louisiana

To my mother, Norma Jean Gibson Hoover, who has been my greatest source of inspiration

Contents

Chapter	Title	Page
1	Experiencing Forgiveness: One Man's Incredible Story	1
2	Letting Go	6
3	Separating Emotions From Actions	15
4	Understanding God's Forgiveness	19
5	Seeing the Importance of Forgiveness	24
6	Forgiving Others	29
7	Forgiving Yourself	42
8	Forgiving: The Steps	49
9	Seeking Forgiveness	60
10	Forgiving When It Doesn't Make Sense	67
11	Reconciling and Trusting After Forgiving	79
12	Inviting a Life of Abundance	83
13	Rebuilding Life After a Broken Trust	87
14	Exercising Forgiveness, Now and Forever	94

Introduction

As Christians, we often believe our lives should be perfect. That we shouldn't struggle with human emotions and that we should automatically be "above" certain things because we profess the name of Christ.

That sounds good in theory. But it isn't realistic.

The truth is that even as we work day by day to become more Christ-like, it is a process. We don't get baptized one day and suddenly all of our problems are washed away in the blood of Jesus.

We realize we are still human, dealing with our human emotions.

This realization can be a stumbling block for many Christians. Once they realize they still are, in fact, dealing with anger and resentment issues, many will give up on the church. They are disappointed that their decision to come to Christ has left them still dealing with things they thought would disappear.

This book will help change that way of thinking. What I've realized in my long career in ministry is that we will always have to deal with our emotions, but we can grow to a level where we are able to address them honestly and ultimately come to terms with them and thus move to a greater level of understanding of who we are and have a greater level of commitment to our Lord.

Dealing with forgiveness on so many levels is part of a Christian's walk. The first level tells us it is difficult for us to truly accept that God forgives us for our transgressions when we refuse to forgive others – and ourselves. The second level tells us forgiveness is important to Christians because we must grow to a point where our hearts are open to love even those who have wronged us in very serious ways. When we are unable to forgive, it means we are stagnant in our Christian journey. Finally, forgiveness is important because it is a part of healing – when we heal, we grow. When we grow, we share the goodness of our Lord.

This is the reason forgiveness is important.

I have spent the past several years dealing with forgiveness in depth. I've presented sermon series on this important topic because I realize people need to have their forgiveness issues addressed in a real – and practical — way. I know from my experiences that unaddressed issues of forgiveness can damage a heart, a home, a ministry, and a mind. I've been able to overcome my own issues dealing with forgiveness, and I have been blessed by God to be able to help countless others do the same.

Whether you are struggling to forgive yourself for something from the past or if you are battling hard feelings you have toward someone who has wronged you, or even if you are having doubts about if God truly has forgiven you, this book can help you tremendously.

Let us heal hearts together.

CHAPTER 1

Experiencing Forgiveness: One Man's Incredible Story

Early one summer morning as he went about his usual routine getting ready for a full workday, a rain of bullets changed Robert Newsome's life forever.

And with it, his heart.

An assassin had been dispatched to kill him. Sounds like a movie, but this actually happened.

Robert tells this story when he talks about the transformative power of forgiveness. It's a story I often reflect on, as it illustrates so plainly the power God has to change our hearts, even in the face of something that human reasoning tells us is unforgivable.

Robert has given me permission to share his story here. A friend he had known for quite some time asked Robert, who was in real estate, about a certain property. Robert gave his honest assessment – he said it was a property that he himself would purchase, if he had the money.

The man, whom we'll call Joe, decided to purchase the building. Joe mismanaged his investment and ended up losing money. He blamed Robert for this loss, as he was not able to accept the reality that he made poor managerial choices concerning his property. He demanded Robert pay him back, despite the fact that Robert had nothing to do with the transaction. Robert, of course, refused. Joe became angry and ultimately hired a local thug to kill Robert.

Robert's friend had put a hit out on him.

GREGORY KIRBY

Robert later learned this man had also been responsible for the deaths of others who had crossed his path.

The episode was quite traumatic for Robert, as you would expect. He fought for his life through more than four hours of surgery and struggled to hold on in a hospital bed, as questions swirled: Why did this happen? Was his family in jeopardy? Was this person coming back to finish the job?

The hit man fired six shots, hitting Robert four times. His body will never be the same as he now suffers with several ailments.

The scars this left on his heart and mind threatened to be there forever, also. Robert grew fearful, as he didn't know if or when his assailant would return. Sounds in the night terrified him. He was afraid to go anywhere, not knowing when another bullet would rip through his body. He didn't trust anyone outside of his immediate family.

He was angry and bitter. His wife, also afraid, left him and moved back to her parents'. Robert's business suffered. The loss of his wife, the damage to his financial stability, and the overall impact on his life turned his heart cold.

He says of that time, "I had always felt that I was a pretty strong Christian. I considered myself close to God."

However when that happened, his faith was shaken. The anger and resentment in his heart stood between him and God and also stood between him and a full recovery.

The bitterness was eating at him.

As the story unfolded, Robert struggled to connect with God and those around him. He ultimately con-

Why Forgiveness Makes Sense

firmed who was behind the shooting – his friend, Joe.

The news shook him, as Joe had been one of the "friends" who had seemed so concerned following the shooting, and even invited Robert to stay at his home during his recovery.

Robert even spoke with the hit man Joe had hired for $2,000.

The hit man asked for forgiveness.

Robert granted it. He even tried to help the hit man get a job and pull his life back together. But still, he struggled with anger. He was having a hard time getting beyond the betrayal of one he considered a friend. Robert was holding onto the hard feelings because he held this man Joe responsible for the shambles his life had become.

But in stepped God's grace. Robert realized one day that he had forgiven not just the young guy who actually fired the shots, but the man who had hired him. With that forgiveness came a newfound freedom: he realized he was no longer afraid. He was no longer afraid to walk around town, or to be seen in public. He was no longer bitter that his wife had run off. He was no longer full of feelings of revenge.

"Forgiveness sets you free," he says now. "If you have any bitterness, it takes bitterness away. It lets you enjoy your life again."

Isn't that powerful? Are you struggling with anger, resentment and bitterness and find they are robbing you of life's very enjoyment? Robert realized something most people don't: forgiveness isn't just for the other person. It's for you. *Don't let others determine your joy*

When we forgive, we release the hold the other person has on our lives. Robert realized holding that anger against those other men wasn't doing anything to

GREGORY KIRBY

them, but it was eating up the very essence of his life.

Robert reclaimed his life with his wife, and went on to do much work within his career, church and community. Joe went to prison.

You may have read this story and you may marvel at God's work in Robert's life, but feel that can't be repeated in your own. I can assure you, it can. No matter how bad the offense that has been committed against you, you can find your way to forgiveness. Robert's story illustrates that.

If he can forgive a man for trying to kill him, you too can forgive others for the hurts they do to you.

Forgiveness is a choice.

Why Forgiveness Makes Sense

"If we practice an eye for an eye and a tooth for a tooth, soon the whole world will be blind and toothless."

— Mahatma Gandhi

AMEN!

GREGORY KIRBY

CHAPTER 2

Letting Go

Hurt and humiliation are never easy companions. Living with that daily pain can slowly eat away a person's soul. Like Robert, you may consider yourself a strong Christian and a basically good person, but tremendous hurt can challenge that.

Many people know — intellectually — that they should forgive another person. But they don't know it emotionally. What do I mean? The simple truth is, forgiveness is not a head issue. It's a heart issue. If you try to reason out why you should not forgive a person, it is easy to have a whole tally sheet of reasons to justify your anger, resentment, and vengeful feelings. But you must realize forgiveness is a choice you make with your heart.

The choice to forgive must start with acknowledging the hurt. You must choose to let go of the anger and all negative feelings.

Again, this isn't about saying the wrong committed against you was all right. Instead, this is about saying you will be all right. It's about choosing to release yourself from the negative emotions that can ruin your life.

But you've got to learn how to let it go. I don't mean just put it on the back burner. I mean let it go. Forgiveness comes from a Greek word that means to release or to be relieved from an obligation or a debt. To be relieved from something that you once had been committed. Whenever a person has paid his debt to society and is released from jail, the paper says forgiven. Whenev-

Why Forgiveness Makes Sense

er individuals go through divorce and the divorce has been granted and the two have been relieved of their obligations to each other, the paper says forgiven. In other words, to forgive means to release someone of what is rightfully their obligation. Many people who are still struggling with forgiveness do so because they have not yet admitted to themselves they are holding a worthless debt they are still trying to collect on. When someone injures or hurts you, the feeling is that this person has created a debt that must somehow be satisfied. Many of us are still mistakenly thinking there is some payment that can be extracted from the offender that will compensate us for our losses. What we are really saying in our thoughts is that we want revenge.

No payment can ease your pain. No settlement can truly lessen your agony. Most of the time the only way to truly settle a debt, the only way to break through that endless cycle of hurt and pain, is forgiveness.

If you are going to be healed, you must take it to God. Jesus says in Matthew 5:44, "Love your enemies."

I know that sounds crazy and most of us have a habit of loving our friends, loving those we are in good standing with, those who we get along with, but Jesus commanded us to go farther. Love your enemies. We'll dissect and study Matthew 5:44 in a later chapter, as it is key to this whole matter of forgiveness. For now, just know that Jesus has commanded us to love those who do us wrong.

That means love those who have hurt you and who have done something against you. It means, in short, have a forgiving spirit. When we have a forgiving spirit, it means we don't wish ill on those who have done ill to us.

This is an important realization. I point this out be-

GREGORY KIRBY

cause oftentimes we are unable to let go of the harsh emotions that wrap around us when we are hurt. I speak from nearly two decades in ministry, but I also speak from personal experience.

My Story

As I worked with others on their issues, I realized I also was dealing with some negative emotions. I had made some poor decisions and had hurt some people. I struggled with the guilt. I tried to calm my emotions and even to make amends, but as I worked on myself, I realized my feelings ran deeper than I cared to admit.

I realized years after I was an adult that some of the hurt I had caused was because I had been hurt. I realized some of the decisions I made were because of my own hard feelings. I realized I held a grudge that started in childhood. I realized I needed to forgive.

I discovered my own journey to forgiveness as I worked with others God had sent to me in ministry. I discovered there were many people who were in the same place as I. So out of that I gained a passion and a desire to want to shed some light on the issues surrounding forgiveness as a way to try to bring healing to people who are hurting because of internal struggles.

When I shed light on their issues, it brought up my own. I grew up feeling like I had to be tough or macho, and that it was not normal for a male to cry or express emotions. As a result, whenever I experienced hurt as a child, I forced it deep within, suffering in silence, hoping it would get better. I became a young person who did not have good coping skills. While on the surface it appeared I was all right, internally, I was a mess.

I grew up in a very dysfunctional family: a family where dad drank all weekend and was not home. If

Why Forgiveness Makes Sense

he did come home, it would be total chaos around the house, including arguing and fighting with our mom. I can't recall ever experiencing a loving, caring environment from my parents. I knew they loved me, but I never remember them saying they loved me or giving me a hug.

I grew resentful. I would go to my friends' homes and see loving relationships, then return home to emptiness.

My mom and dad finally divorced when I was in seventh grade. I was angry about that. I remember literally begging God to allow my parents to get back together. Home may have been unhappy and chaotic when they were together, but at least they were together, and in my mind, at that time, that was better than the new reality of divorce. I held onto anger and frustration and felt letdown and disappointed by my parents. I even felt like God had let me down.

That carried over into adulthood.

After the divorce, I felt abandoned by both my parents, my mother because she left and my father because he was never available. I was living with my father and pretty much raising myself, as he would be gone for days at a time.

I was an unhappy, unfulfilled person. I probably suffered from low self esteem. I felt I always had to try hard to fit in or try to be accepted by other people and would often times go well above and beyond what was necessary to fit in. I desperately wanted to feel connected to others, to feel the love or acceptance that evaded me at home. My efforts to fit in, no matter what, ultimately led to more hurt and pain because I realized others were not giving me the same effort and interest. I would put my own desires and interests on hold to

GREGORY KIRBY

satisfy the need of the person I wanted to be my friend. If that person wanted something, I would try to deliver it. I was determined to win affection.

But nobody could live up to the expectations I laid out. Nobody could fill the void in my life, and the result was a constant stream of broken relationships – friendships, romantic involvements.

Even as I struggled to connect with others, I refused to let them get too close, after all, my parents had been the closest, and they had left me. It was a counterproductive cycle. I worked hard to get people to like me, but I worked even harder to try to keep them at arm's length. After dealing with so much hurt and frustration in relationships, I didn't want to open up. I started going through emotional changes. I tried to make excuses for the way I was feeling, trying to convince myself I was all right and normal, and all the time I knew I was not.

For years, I was unable to admit I was hurting. I refused to acknowledge the impact my parents' divorce had on me, and therefore, I could not let go of the hard feelings. The result was a life of destructive tendencies. In high school, at times I was the over achiever because I was determined to win love, at any cost to my personal self. Then in college, I chose another way to win love: I would succumb to the pressure to fit in. I drank, experimented with alcohol, and joined a fraternity. While I enjoy my fraternity, I am now able to admit I joined it, not because of any real desire to do community service or anything so noble, but because I thought this was a place I could finally have real connections, after all, these brothers had sworn to be connected.

My hurts led to other life decisions, including a marriage. I left college and ended up going to the military

Why Forgiveness Makes Sense

and getting married, almost impulsively. Not because of any of the real foundational principles that marriage should be built on, but because of the social and emotional void that this person filled in my life. But when those needs failed to be met, I began to be haunted by my past and again I felt unhappy, unfulfilled, unloved, and betrayed. All those dysfunctions I had known as a kid and as a young adult came together. It was at the breakup of this marriage that I began to acknowledge what was going on with me.

Through those life experiences and my work in ministry, I realize now I was struggling because I failed to forgive. I was holding a grudge. I loved my parents dearly, but I was still blaming them for not keeping my family together. Because I loved them, I refused to acknowledge my baggage until it became too heavy.

For me, letting go of this baggage meant a new level of closeness to God and a new freedom to pursue healthy relationships. I had to decide that my parents did the best they could with what they had and release them from the negative emotional hold. I had to make a choice that I would no longer allow my life to be guided by anger, resentment, and the guilt at feeling those emotions. I forgave them for the dysfunctional life they gave me and I forgave myself for the choices I made to that point.

We'll talk in upcoming chapters about other steps to forgiveness, but I hope you now realize the importance of this step of letting go. Until you let go of the baggage from the past – no matter how much you think you deserve to feel a certain way – you can't forgive. And if you can't forgive, you can't truly live.

GREGORY KIRBY

I shared my story so you will see that I don't speak from some detached reality, but from a very real desire to see forgiveness work in your life, because I know how destructive a lack of forgiveness can be. I want you to experience the wholeness forgiveness brings.

This is why Jesus said love your enemies. He said bless those who hurt you. Pray for those who do you wrong. Isn't that the opposite of what most of us do? When is the last time you attempted to love somebody you know was plotting your downfall? Someone who is your enemy? Love your enemy. Bless those who curse you. The only way you're going to make it through is you've got to take it to God. God will give you the strength to make the choice to let go and forgive.

In my nearly 20 years in ministry, I've seen hatred and hard feelings do some bad things. I've seen these negative emotions literally destroy lives of people who refused to forgive. They refused to let go.

But just as I've seen that, I have also seen – in Robert's case and scores of others – how letting go can give a person a new life.

How do you let go?

Letting go of negative emotions can be a difficult task for some, but it's not impossible. Here are some steps if you are having trouble letting go of hurt from your past.

1. Recognize the negative feelings. Many people deny the anger, resentment, or heartache that burns within. They try to cover it up and pretend all is well. The first step on your road to forgiveness is to acknowledge that these feelings dwell in your heart.

2. Realize the negative feelings are not helping you. Some people hold onto hard feelings because they feel

Why Forgiveness Makes Sense

they have a right to do so. They believe they are somehow getting back at the person with whom they are angry. If you are one who thinks that way, you must realize the hard feelings are not about the other person. They are about you. They are making life harder for you. How? Negative emotions increase stress levels, can raise blood pressure, and cause strain. They decrease the quality of life of the one who has those negative emotions.

3. Know that you can not move forward if you let negative emotions hold you back. It is impossible to live your life fully if you are constantly wrapped up in emotions that block your joy. You cannot fully embrace your ministry, your family, your career, or any other pursuit when you are in this negative state of mind.

4. Choose to release. Finally, after acknowledging your emotional state, you must make a conscious choice to change it. When you feel the anger about the past returning, choose not to dwell on it. Pray for a change of heart and actively work for that change by redirecting your thoughts. You may not be able to choose which thoughts enter your mind, but you can choose which ones take up residence there.

Letting go is the first stage of forgiveness. Now that you've acknowledged your emotions and have chosen to no longer allow them to dominate your thoughts, you are ready to move forward.

GREGORY KIRBY

"To err is human, to forgive, divine."

— Alexander Pope

Why Forgiveness Makes Sense

CHAPTER 3

Separating Emotions From Actions

We must face the fact that nobody escapes this life without some hurt. It's as sure as death and taxes. Often, those closest to us can hurt us the most. Sometimes the hurt is small, sometimes it's immense.

Once a person has taken the first step and has made a choice to go down the road of forgiveness, he or she must come face to face with this realization: How do you keep your resolve to let go when the hurt is still there?

The first thing to remember is that you do have control. Often we believe we are victims of our emotions, and so we lash out and do unhealthy things because we think we can't help it. We fall into the trap of thinking, "That's just the way I am."

Paul addresses this in Romans 7 when he says those things he should do, he does not and those that he should not do, those are the things he does. He shows us here that the human nature alone will not necessarily do what is right. In other words, our natural inclination may be to yield to unhealthy notions and reactions. The flesh does not take kindly to being slighted or offended. We want to get back at somebody, and get back at that person hard! We want to hold grudges. We want to retaliate, and often with a vengeance. But that's why we seek God. We cannot forgive without seeking heaven.

But forgiveness requires that we renew our minds. Paul tells us in Romans 12:2, "Be ye transformed by the renewing of your mind."

That means we must elevate ourselves. That comes from a true kinship with Jesus Christ. When we take on his spirit, we are consciously behaving like him. To do so, it requires turning our lives over to Jesus and inviting him into our hearts. Then, when the natural being – the flesh – would seek an eye for an eye, the Christian spirit seeks instead to look for other means. We die to our natural selves and allow our rebirth in Jesus to govern our very hearts.

Yes, it is impossible to overcome the hard feelings when we work on our own. But when we invite Jesus into our hearts and listen for that still, small voice of the Holy Spirit, we find victory over that anger easier.

We must remember we choose our realities. If we focus on the negative, we will reap the negative. That is why Paul urges us to be transformed by this renewal of our minds. When I renew my mind, I make it new. I change it. I make it better.

This renewal helps us emotionally, but it also helps us spiritually, because forgiveness is a spiritual issue. Most people consider it only an emotional concern. But Christians know better. When we use God's word to address our issues of guilt, resentment, and anger, we open ourselves to new possibilities. Even as we remember forgiveness is a spiritual matter, we must deal with our human emotions.

■

How to face negative emotions:

1. Remember your decision to let go. Keep reminding yourself of the choice you made in the previous chapter to let go of those emotions that do not benefit you.

2. Draw on your relationship with Christ. Whether you are a long-time believer or a new Christian, lean

Why Forgiveness Makes Sense

on Jesus. Pray for a change of heart. Pray that the hard feelings dissolve from your consciousness and that a spirit of peace concerning the matter replaces it.

3. Consume positive words. Read Biblical scriptures and motivational works that promote good feelings. Choose reading materials that enhance your decision, not materials that compromise it.

4. Seek a spiritual partner. Find someone who can encourage you. If you are comfortable doing so, share your story with this person and ask that he or she pray with you.

Finding closure about the particular event that hurt you can also be a powerful tool in overcoming it. One way to gain that closure is to write a letter. Write a letter to the person who hurt you, telling why the experience hurt you and how it affected you. Then share with this person that you have forgiven him or her. That's right. Write the words, "I forgive you."

Now, you don't have to mail it, if you don't want. This exercise isn't about whether the person receives the note. It's about you and what the note does for you. The important part is that you write the letter and get your emotions out. This allows you to get beyond the emotions and resolve issues that may be circulating in your subconscious.

Closure helps us move on.

GREGORY KIRBY

"**Love can turn the cottage into a golden palace.**"

— German proverb

Love heals all Wounds!

Why Forgiveness Makes Sense

CHAPTER 4

Understanding God's Forgiveness

For many people, it's not just a struggle of how to forgive others. It's a struggle to understand how God can forgive us. Some people look at forgiveness with their limited vision, their human eyes. And they judge God's forgiveness with this view. "I can't forgive so and so for what he did to me, so how can God forgive me for all I've done?" is a common question I hear in ministry.

Because of this confusion, many people stay away from church, ministry, and the commitment to a real spiritual journey. They can't imagine a God who can forgive their transgressions.

But when we understand God's forgiveness, we can accept that his love for us knows no bounds and no matter what we've done in the past, he can forgive us. All we must do is ask.

∎

How can we receive God's forgiveness?

Make no mistake. God's forgiveness of our sins is expensive. It's a price we could never pay. It's a gift that the Lord gives to us because his son Jesus paid the price for us. The Bible tells us that there can be no forgiveness of sin without the shedding of blood. Jesus allowed his blood to be shed for your sins and mine. When he died, he paid it forward. When we seek Jesus, his blood covers the wrong we have done and the mistakes we have made. First John 1:9 tells us, "If we confess our sins, he is faithful and just to forgive us our sins."

That is the beauty of salvation. We get a gift of forgiveness. All we have to do is ask. When we understand this, it frees us of the emotional bondage guilt can have over us. I've met many people who have felt helpless and hopeless and they have ruined their lives as a result. They have felt they could never be free of their pasts, so they kept making poor decisions. At the core of their despair was a feeling that God would not forgive them, so why should they try to do and be better?

That is wrong thinking. No matter what horrible thing you have done, it is never too late to receive God's forgiveness. Yes, you may have to pay the earthly penalty for the bad decisions of your past – repaying society, making it up to loved ones, suffering the loss of a relationship, etc. – but once God forgives you, there are no more eternal penalties. He forgives and forgets. Your sins are tossed into the sea of forgetfulness.

Does that mean you will not have to live with the consequences of your actions? No, it doesn't. Because God gives us choice – free will – he also allows us to see the results of our actions. That means sometimes our poor decisions have long lasting consequences. That means if you made poor decisions as a young adult, you may see the evidence of them years later. Forgiveness doesn't mean we don't have to deal with what we have done. Forgiveness means it's no longer held against us.

In the Old Testament of the Bible, the children of Israel made animal sacrifices when they wanted to seek God's forgiveness. That was a visual reminder of what they had done. But when Jesus died on the cross, his shed blood was our reminder and our redemption.

God wants nothing to stand between us and him.

Why Forgiveness Makes Sense

When we refuse to seek his forgiveness, we are creating a barrier. We are allowing a divide to separate us. And when we refuse to believe that God can – and does - forgive us, then we are calling him a liar.

Is that what you want to do? Have you been calling God a liar in your actions? When we feel we are unforgiven by God, that hurts us. That sends us down self destructive paths and it makes our lives unnecessarily difficult.

While we as humans see "big" sins and "little" sins, in God's eyes, all sins are the same. That is why no sin is "too big" for Him to forgive. Why? Because his son died to cover all the sins of humanity. Now, are you still feeling that what you have done is "too big" for God to forgive?

If so, get on your knees and say this prayer:

Prayer for God's forgiveness:
"Dear Heavenly Father, I thank you for the beauty of life and for the forgiveness you have granted me. Thank you for sending your son to die so that I may have forgiveness. I accept this gift, knowing I can never earn it, but can still receive it because you love me. Please give me the peace to go forward, secure in the knowledge that you have forgiven me. In Jesus's name, amen."

Jesus gave us a perfect prayer in Matthew 6:9-13. It is:

"Our father, which art in heaven, hallowed be thy name. Thy kingdom come. Thy will be done in earth as it is in heaven. Give us this day, our daily bread. And forgive us our debts, as we forgive our debtors. And lead us not into temptation, but deliver us from evil.

For thine is the kingdom, the power and the glory, forever. Amen."

Here, it is a model prayer when we don't know how else to pray or what to pray. Notice that even in this model, Jesus clearly shows the need for forgiveness by including references. He could have easily included any number of other things, but it is forgiveness that is among the things he wants to bring attention to in this passage.

He tells us here, as he shares throughout scripture, that God forgives us as we forgive those who need our forgiveness.

Why Forgiveness Makes Sense

"Father, forgive them."

— Jesus Christ

CHAPTER 5

Seeing the Importance of Forgiveness

Remember when I said earlier that forgiveness is a choice? The Word bears witness. It's a choice you must make with your heart. In Mark 11:25, it says, if you are standing praying, if you hold anything against anyone, forgive them so that your Father in heaven will be able to forgive you. When Jesus was on the cross, He didn't just say to the thieves, listen, I forgive you. He said, "Father, forgive them." Even if the other person does not repent. Somehow it's in some of our minds that people need to earn forgiveness from us.

We think forgiveness is about the offenders. Forgiveness is about the offended.

Jesus gave us an example of how to forgive when He prayed for those who harmed Him. "Father, forgive them."

We'll talk more about this in later chapters, but Jesus was showing us that we must have a role in forgiveness.

Now that we have realized that God can and will forgive us for our sins, we have a responsibility to extend forgiveness to others.

Why is forgiveness so important?

It helps us show our faith and grow in our relationship with God. Think about it. Is it easier to show that you haven't forgiven someone or that you have? The former, of course. It's much easier to walk around in

Why Forgiveness Makes Sense

a huff and to make it obvious to everyone around that you are holding a grudge. How does that help others see the light that is within you? How does that show your relationship with God?

Now, look at the opposite scenario. What happens if you show kindness to the one who hurt you or what happens when you offer prayers for instead of curses against the one who offended you? What happens then is that you are able to let evidence of God in your life show. You are then a witness for the redemptive power of our Lord. When we forgive, it helps us grow as believers.

It protects our hearts. That's right, forgiving others keeps our hearts open and soft. When we hold onto unforgiveness, our hearts become hard and brittle. Forgiveness helps us to steer clear of bitter resentment that can crop up when we dwell on how badly someone else has treated us.

It's what Jesus commands. We can reason all day as to why we should forgive, but perhaps there is one answer that covers all other answers: it's what Jesus told us to do. In Matthew 18:21 and 22, when Peter asked how many times should we forgive? Jesus said multiple times upon multiple times. Jesus was telling us that our forgiveness should never be exhausted.

Forgiving those who wrong us can make our lives so much easier. We are on this earth but for a short time, and if we allow hard feelings to consume that time, we lose. We have denied our hurt so much that we don't even realize our own stubborn desire to hold onto pain is the reason we are hurting. Sounds crazy?

It is very much real. I have a dear church member who has a beautiful heart. She is kind, considerate, and

GREGORY KIRBY

is a hard worker. But for the longest time, she did not realize she was limiting her true potential.

She tried to dull the hurt and pain of her childhood with alcohol and drugs. The result was a life of one wrong decision after the other. Her children suffered, her self-esteem suffered, her heart suffered. Her pain stemmed from a childhood where her father seemed to favor other children. Her father had multiple families, and the woman I speak of felt lost in the shuffle. She felt she was always competing to win her father's affection and that nothing she did was ever good enough.

The result was a life spent searching for that acceptance. She was angry and hurt.

As she grew up, she packed away the hurt she felt and that produced the destructive tendencies that sent her to drugs and the alcohol. I am pleased to say she was able to overcome her addictions, face her true issues, and allow a forgiving spirit to free her from her pain.

This is an example of why forgiveness is essential.

■

Forgiveness isn't as embedded into our culture as it should be. Sure, we all want it when it's in our favor, but the exercise of it is a rarer event. That is why when we see true forgiveness in its glory, it's a powerful display.

A tragic event happened in October of 2006, when a gunman burst into a tiny, one-room school house in a rural part of Pennsylvania, called Nickel Mines, in an Amish community. He lined up nearly a dozen girls, shooting them, killing five, before taking his own life. What happened next is almost unbelievable, except we know it is factual because we saw true evidence of it.

That community – along with the girls' families – extended love to the family of the man who had com-

Why Forgiveness Makes Sense

mitted this horrific act. They visited the man's family, offering prayers, food and condolences.

What an amazing act of forgiveness? Those people, who had just had their young stolen away from them, were able to reach out to the family of the man who had done the killing. They recognized that man's family was suffering, too. Those Amish families chose to forgive, because they knew that is what God would have them to do.

Sometimes forgiving means being bigger than our individual pain and our individual circumstances.

The effort by that Amish community not only helped to begin healing for the people there, but it served to remind us in the rest of America just how important forgiveness is. It also showed us that there is nothing so bad that it can't be forgiven.

I often wonder how forgiveness might be used to solve other social ills that plague us today. We can't turn on the news or open a newspaper without seeing the results of lives where the motivating factors are grudges, resentment, and anger.

What of the wars going on in the world? Might a bit of forgiveness change the outcome of a whole generation and of generations to come? If we are able to put aside our egos and our bitterness, what problem can we not solve? If we follow the example of the Bible, and the example of those Amish families, we can write a blueprint for a whole new world.

What if we instead used love and forgiveness to solve what ails us? Forgiveness starts with the individual. What part will you play in changing your home, your church, your community, or even – the world?

GREGORY KIRBY

"Doing an injury puts you below your enemy. Revenging one makes you but even with him. Forgiving it sets you above him."

— Benjamin Franklin

CHAPTER 6
Forgiving Others

I've had numerous people to sit before me with anger, bitterness – even hatred – burning in their hearts. I've had couples to come for counseling as a last resort, with one partner dragging the other there. They've outlined their partners' transgressions. They've told me why their marriage is so broken they feel surely divorce is in order. And often, one partner or the other is almost sitting on the edge of the seat, waiting for me to beat up on the other partner for the problems of the marriage. And some of the things done, some of the acts committed by the partner in question, are quite bad. The transgressions have been everything one can imagine.

But as I work with them to get through their problems, I bring them to a point of recognizing the role of forgiveness.

At first, the partner who has been wronged (and often, both partners have been wronged because a fight isn't just about one person), is resistant to granting forgiveness to the person who did the wrong.

"Why should I forgive this other person?" is the question.

Understand, the person who feels betrayed and hurt often cannot see why he or she has to "give up," yet another thing. In that person's eyes, he or she has already had to "give up" the dream he or she cherished, a dream that was dashed when the partner committed the betrayal. Now, I'm sitting before them asking the betrayed partner to "give up," these emotions he or she feels a right to hold onto.

It almost seems unfair to the person who feels hurt.

But I persist. I persist because I know forgiveness is about more than the other person. Forgiveness is about the person who has been hurt. We've already discussed the importance of letting go of transgressions. You know granting forgiveness isn't so much about freeing the other person, but it's about freeing yourself.

Forgiveness is something all of us want, but very few of us are willing to give. All of us want others to forgive us; we want people to be understanding when it comes to our faults and our failures. But when it comes to us forgiving others, we are very reluctant. We are hesitant. Jesus makes it clear in his Word that forgiveness is something you cannot have unless you are willing to give it. Forgiveness has to be a two-way street. You have to be willing to give it, in order to get it.

The Bible says we can't rid ourselves of emotional pain and side effects unless we are willing to forgive. Forgiveness makes sense. Unresolved anger keeps us from moving forward because it locks us in a time machine and freezes us on the exact wrong someone has done to us. It causes us to have fear of any future injuries and makes us unwilling to move ahead and go to another level in a relationship. It damages our ability to bond, not just with those who have hurt us, but with others we see as threats because of our experience. I know some folks who were once married and are now single. They are single, not because they can't find somebody, but because the injury was so severe, the wound was so serious, that it has frozen them on that exact event and it has literally paralyzed them from taking the risk of any future injury.

Why Forgiveness Makes Sense

The hurts are by no way only limited to our close family. I've seen hurts under other circumstances having similar effects on people. I know of people who were so damaged by something that happened at work that they held onto that hurt and anger and they are still struggling in their professional lives.

I've seen people who used to be good, faithful members — workers — of a church, yet, they don't want to get too caught up in the church where I pastor. Why? They tell me, "Well, pastor, I don't want to get too involved. At my other church, I was involved and I had a bad experience."

What they fail to see is they are holding onto an unforgiving spirit and are robbing themselves of the joy of moving forward, of getting involved. I know the people I've worked with and those I've helped to move beyond their pain are not the only ones. Is it possible that you are in the same position? What offense are you stuck on? What pain are you nursing?

■

What does forgiving another mean?

Let's start with the best example we can find. And that is Jesus. You remember, don't you, when Jesus was hanging on the cross in Luke 23:34, and he said, "Father, forgive them; for they know not what they do."

What Jesus was really saying was: "I release them."

Jesus wasn't saying they didn't do the thing, but he was saying, my heart is troubled and I'm truly saddened because they don't know what they are doing. That's the same process you must go through if you are to be free.

Forgiving another person doesn't say what they did was right. It doesn't even say you two will be friends afterward. It does not deny that there was a hurt. But what it does say is that you no longer have ill will toward that person.

We sometimes think forgiveness means we must restore the broken relationship or we must go back to where things were. Forgiveness doesn't have to mean that. Some relationships will never be restored to what they once were – and that is all right. For instance, if someone was abusive to you and threatened your life, forgiving that person doesn't mean you will put yourself back in the same position of being abused or threatened. God is the lord of light and of love, and it is not his wish that any of his children are abused or harmed. He gives us common sense and good judgment so that once we learn lessons, we don't make the decisions that put us back in those positions. And if we learn that a certain circumstance is dangerous to us, he doesn't expect us to ignore reason and go back there.

Impact of Forgiveness

In Matthew 18:21-35, Jesus shares a parable of an unforgiving servant. In this familiar scripture, a servant goes before the king owing quite a lot. Well, the king is ready to mete out an appropriate fine to have the debt met – the man, his wife and his children would all be sold. Well, the servant begged and pleaded for mercy. The king, feeling compassion, granted the request and forgave the debt and sent the man on his way.

The man, in turn, came across a fellow servant who owed him a small amount. The servant, who had been forgiven of his debt, refused the fellow servant's pleadings for mercy and cast him into prison because of the unforgiven debt.

The result of this was the king heard about the way

Why Forgiveness Makes Sense

the servant behaved and took him to task, this time without forgiveness.

This illustration makes it clear that unless we forgive others, we can't get God's forgiveness. So the impact of our forgiving of others is that God is then open to forgive us.

Forgiveness Is a Fresh Start

Forgiveness means a new beginning. That means you start where you are – with all that has happened – and you go from there. Sometimes, that could mean a relationship that was damaged by hurt and broken trust is restored to be even stronger in its maturity. Sometimes that means you as the one who has forgiven may reach out to the one you chose to forgive. Sometimes it means you assess how the situation came about and you make choices that would protect you from being in that same position again.

Must I Forget If I Forgive?

Forgiveness is about forgetting. I know the conventional wisdom of the world is that we forgive but we don't forget, and that is according to our human understanding. We may say we forgive, but if we are holding onto the remembrance of the wrong, we haven't truly forgiven, not according to the model we see in the Bible.

Here, I will bring in a popular scripture. First Corinthians 13 tells us that love keeps no record of wrong doing. In other words, love is forgiveness. If we say we love God and know that God is love, then we must act in that love. And if we say we forgive but we don't forget, then we are not speaking truth.

GREGORY KIRBY

In our Christian walk, what we will find is that forgiveness means forgetting. That means when we truly forgive, we don't bring up the old transgressions someone has committed against us because we don't hold them in our hearts. In Romans 12:18, Paul advises that we should live peaceably with others, whenever we can. That makes it clear that we can't hold onto all the junk that would make that difficult.

We can't look to ourselves to "settle the score" when someone hurts us. We leave that up to God. In that same chapter of Romans, verse 17, it tells us not to repay evil with evil. We can't be in the business of making people pay for what they do to us. That is God's department, and he can do it better than we can. That is why when we truly choose to forgive, we know we are out of the vengeance business.

Talking Through Forgiveness

Certainly infidelity within marital relationships is one of the key reasons many spouses are unwilling to forgive. This is one of the reasons couples come to me for counseling, especially when they feel like nothing else can be done.

But I am here to tell you that even with such a trying circumstance, forgiveness has a place – if parties are willing to be open. I remember one case in which one spouse had engaged in a sexual relationship with someone outside of the marriage. Of course this caused their marriage to be quite chaotic. The wife didn't want to talk because she was ashamed. The husband didn't want to talk because he was ashamed. Often when we aren't able to talk through our hurts, it only makes things worse.

This couple was experiencing raw emotions. They

Why Forgiveness Makes Sense

were in emotional bondage because they refused to communicate. Oftentimes, when we have been hurt, we have been in a terrible storm, but we don't have anywhere to go. We have no shelter. We don't have anybody we can trust. So we end up keeping things to ourselves. That's what this couple was doing.

Each spouse was keeping the strain and hurt inside but that wasn't doing anybody any good because the hurt was manifesting itself in their lives. They were strangers to each other, each going about a separate life, aching because of past anger. While they were technically married, that's where the connection ended, as they lived separately off and on for quite a while. They would move in together and move out. Then repeat the process. Their children were hurt and confused. Family members didn't know what was wrong or how to help.

No self help book can get us to the point of recovery once we have been badly bruised and wounded like that and are not willing to see beyond those feelings. Lots of folks are walking around in silence because they have not grasped the spiritual principle of forgiveness.

We've already found in this book that we can't "even" the score on our own. No matter how much pain we try to inflict in retaliation, that won't ease our emotional burdens. That's why we must let Jesus be a part of the healing. We find comfort in Christ Jesus. That is why spiritual counseling grants a different perspective than the counseling the world gives. The world may say a couple cannot recover from infidelity, but when we approach the issue with a spiritual mind, we open ourselves to the possibility.

Such was the case with this couple. We worked through their issues and their hearts opened to forgiveness. They became willing to communicate. They put aside their anger and resentment and stepped away from their desires to each "get even" with the other.

Forgiveness found a place for healing in their marriage. What helped this couple is that they were willing to build spiritual relationships with those who are close to them in the faith and then allow those spiritual friends to embrace them and be a source of encouragement. I was one of their spiritual friends. But they realized they had to surround themselves with other people of faith who could support their desire to reconcile.

Find a spiritual support system that does not take the world's view that you repay hurt with hurt. Choose, instead, a spiritual guide who encourages you to let Jesus settle the score as you find new ways to communicate.

Forgiveness Eases Pain

Psalms 147:3 tells us that God heals the broken hearted and bandages their wounds. That is significant when you think about it from a spiritual perspective. When we are bruised and wounded, God says he will bandage up those wounds and protect them. Even as he bandages the wounds, God brings healing.

That is what happened for the couple I told you about earlier, and it can happen for you. God heals wounds. We must remember, though, that just like physical healing, spiritual healing can take time. When you have been badly wounded, sometimes it requires a period of silence and solitude.

You may not automatically feel healed. For instance, if you have a broken leg, there may be a period where you must be still. After that, you have to get up and make yourself work through the hurt. Force yourself to do this work. That is why it's good to have other people around to help. When we are physically hurt, we

Why Forgiveness Makes Sense

go to the physical therapist because the doctor knows we won't work through the pain by ourselves. Choose a spiritual friend to help you through your emotional hurts.

When I was seven or eight years old and we were on our grandfather's farm, we were playing with some sharp axes. I fell on one of them and cut my arm quite badly. That's been forty years ago, but I still have the scar. Even sometimes with emotional wounds and hurts, even when we are healed, we have to realize there are scars still left that we have to make a conscious effort to face properly. We can either look at the scar and remember our hurt and stew over it all over again, or we can look at the scar and move on and rejoice.

With the married couple, the fact that nobody wanted to talk made it almost impossible for them to be restored to a healthy relationship and fellowship. Hurt can cause us to nearly shut down. But when we make up our minds to deal with our issues, we are then open to healing.

Forgiving the one who hurt you may not immediately take away the pain, as we've just discussed. But that choice to forgive is the only way to get beyond the pain. It's like the wound we talked in an above example. As you start to take care of the wound, it gradually heals, until one day, it doesn't hurt anymore. You may find too, that the wound that used to occupy so much of your attention gets only an occasional glance. So it is with your emotional wounds under the care of forgiveness. Sometimes, through our prayers, God grants us the immediate release from the pain. Other times, we realize that by working on our wounds – going through the forgiveness process – we will gain relief from the hurt.

I have seen many instances where tending to the

wounds not only eased the pain, but created a new joy. In many instances where the hurts are finally addressed, those involved in the situations are able to move forward in a way that enhances the lives of all involved.

I worked with a family in which the parents had passed away and the siblings lashed out at each other in their grief. Some of the siblings accused the others of persuading the parents to show favor by giving them something "extra." This happens often in families where parents die and then fights about property, inheritance, and money ensue. Feelings will be hurt, accusations made, and the result often is resentment.

In this particular case, the hurt resulted in a rift in the family so wide that the siblings stopped speaking. In fact, the sisters and brothers didn't speak to each other for years. They each went about their lives as if the others did not exist.

Their children were not able to play with each other and build relationships.

These siblings had severe hurts and pains they were covering, pretending to be tough; pretending that they were OK. They missed being a part of each other's lives and missed being able to be of comfort to each other following the parental loss.

This continued until one approached me and asked for my help. The family member admitted they were all struggling and didn't think they would be able to move on with their lives until their family issue was resolved.

God used me to help bring the family members together in a way to create healing and restoration.

It turns out that nobody had persuaded the parents to favor one sibling over the other. That was just a per-

Why Forgiveness Makes Sense

ception that arose during a very stressful and emotional time. The sibling who made the accusation was just not able to think clearly while dealing with the loss of parents and once the accusation was out, words were said and the situation escalated to the painful point of them not speaking.

But once these siblings tended the wounds, they were able to have a better life. The sides came back together to give each other comfort and support.

Their children were able to associate and they each gained pleasure from being a part of a healthy family once again.

When they worked on their wounds, they found that communication was what they needed. In our sessions, they spoke honestly with each other, voicing their individual truths. It's important to remember that when you forgive a person, it does not mean you can't be honest about how you feel.

Being honest about the emotions involved in the situation helps you move beyond the hurt.

As a result of their honest communication, these family members were able to share without anyone being judgmental. They were able to accept each other's emotions.

That family is a success story I enjoy sharing because they were able to become just as close as they were before the strife separated them.

When we refuse this forgiveness process, we allow that hurt to fester, and, in some instances, grow bigger. Have you ever met someone who experienced a hurt a long time ago, but they talk about it as if it happened just that morning? They have nursed the hurt. Tend to the wounds and the hurt will take care of itself.

Hurt cannot grow if we don't allow it to do so. When

GREGORY KIRBY

you're ready to ease the pain of hurt, you are ready to let forgiveness do its job.

Forgiveness gives a new perspective.

Why Forgiveness Makes Sense

"Forgiveness is a gift you give yourself."

— Unknown

CHAPTER 7
Forgiving Yourself

Many of us are harder on ourselves than we are on others. We are more critical of ourselves than of others. That can be positive and negative. It can be positive when it challenges us to strive for our best. It can be detrimental when we hold ourselves up to unfair and unattainable standards.

When we are hard on ourselves, we tend to hold onto and grieve over our past mistakes. I know in my life, I feel badly whenever I make mistakes. Whenever I blow it, I sometimes beat myself up. In those instances, I may mope for a long time or chide myself over even small infractions. Oftentimes, it's when I am unduly hard on myself that I find myself suffering in silence. The truth is, it's hard for us to let other people know we are hurting. I've had others to hurt me and to wrong me, but I must admit, I've caused more pain to myself than others have caused me. It has been hard for me to learn to forgive myself, but I have; that has helped quite a bit.

Because I now know the process of forgiving myself, I am able to bring myself back on course when I recognize a pattern of behavior that suggests I am holding onto negative emotions.

When you recognize your own patterns of negative behavior, you will more easily recognize an unforgiving spirit within. When you recognize what is going on, you are empowered to change it.

Most of us can quote scriptures about forgiveness. We can throw out First John 1:9, "If we confess our sins, he is faithful and just to forgive us our sins."

Why Forgiveness Makes Sense

But we think it takes more than that. In essence, we feel we have a higher standard for forgiving ourselves than God does for forgiving us! We want to put ourselves through all sorts of hoops, yet God tells us that His forgiveness is available just at our request.

How is it that we can hold sins against ourselves even when God hasn't? God is quick to forgive us, but we are slow to forgive ourselves. We beat ourselves up, thinking about how dumb, selfish, and stupid we have been. We lament, wishing we could just start all over again and go back in time.

At first, as you recognize your need to forgive yourself, you may still feel angry with yourself. You may even still feel hurt or sad. That's a part of the process. But realize you can't stay there. That's where too many of us get stuck; you must move beyond that. You've got to regain your freedom. You must remember you have something at stake. Your eternal destiny is not at stake, but your daily victory is. You are saved and on your way to heaven if you've accepted Jesus as your savior, but until you are free, until you forgive yourself, your daily victory is in peril. If you're going to be free, you've got to learn how to talk to yourself, because Satan will always whisper in one ear about how undeserving you are. Satan is going to tell you that you can never overcome that. Satan is going to tell you this will haunt you for the rest of your life. But on the other hand, you've got to learn how to encourage yourself. Remember Isaiah 53:5, which says Jesus was wounded for our transgressions and we are healed because of his sacrifice.

That means we are healed from physical and emotional pain. Healed from guilt and anger. You don't have to continue to beat yourself up. You can be free and you can move forward.

GREGORY KIRBY

The reason we have difficulty moving forward is because we tear ourselves apart, for we are outright ashamed of the choices we have made. One of Jesus's disciples had the same problem: he tore himself apart. Why? Because he blew it. He messed up. He outright lied and disappointed Jesus. It was hard for him to forgive himself. You remember Peter. Jesus told Peter that Peter would betray him and Peter was adamant, "I will not!" He even said he would go to prison for Jesus, or even die for Him.

Yet, when it got down to it, Peter did exactly what Jesus had predicted he would do. He denied even knowing Jesus.

You know the story: Jesus told Peter that before the cock crows three times, Peter would betray Jesus by denying Him three times. Each time someone asked Peter if he knew Jesus, Peter denied it, angrily even. "I don't know Him!"

By the time Peter made his third denial, the cock crowed and Jesus lifted His eyes and looked at Peter, who then remembered Jesus's prediction.

Peter cried bitterly. Can you imagine the shame, the pain, the hurt it caused Peter for him to disappoint Jesus? Yet Peter went on to become one of the most known apostles. Once he was able to let go of the anger he held toward himself, once he was able to release himself from the shame of his betrayal, he was able to rise above it and do great work.

That too can be our story. Once we move beyond our mistakes and stop beating ourselves up over them, we too can go on to do great work. We can be examples of spiritual growth.

Sure, there are some times we do bad things out of ill intentions. But there are other times when our inten-

Why Forgiveness Makes Sense

tions were good or when we didn't set out to do harm. We look back and say, "Had I known it would cause the pain, the hurt, the anger it has caused, I would not have done it. If I could do it all over again, I would do some things differently."

We do things differently by not repeating the same mistakes. Often when we are unforgiving to ourselves, we are unable to stop making the same mistakes. And so we become even angrier with ourselves. It's a cycle to which we see no end – until we seek God and ask for His help in softening our hearts.

God doesn't expect us to be perfect. And just as Jesus knew Peter would mess up, so it is today. God knows we will mess up sometimes. That's why He gave us a way out. A way to get back. First John 2:1 says essentially: "I prefer that you not sin, but if you do, you have an advocate in Jesus."

You have somebody who will go to bat for you, and that is Jesus. He is your substitute, your vindicator. That means you don't have to beat yourself up. Jesus has taken your punishment. Your mess-up did not catch God off guard. Peter had to learn to forgive himself. We have to do the same. What are you still blaming yourself for which it is too late for you to do anything about anyway? What are you still holding against yourself that truly is water under the bridge? What is preventing you from moving forward and doing great work for God? God can't use you, until you let it go and forgive yourself.

Another reason we struggle with forgiving ourselves is that we have the wrong idea about forgiveness. We struggle with forgiving ourselves because somehow society has made us believe that in order for us to forgive ourselves, it must be somehow earned. We feel that somehow, we need to be extra good in order to make up for the bad we have done. One of our problems is that we have not made the distinction between being forgiven and feeling forgiven. There is a difference between feeling like you are forgiven and actually being forgiven. That goes back to our understanding of God's forgiveness of us, which we discuss elsewhere in this book. Sometimes it takes our emotions a while to catch up with reality. We may sometimes just start to feel forgiven by God long after He has actually forgiven us. That translates to how we forgive ourselves.

What you are really struggling with is the overwhelming guilt that has been caused by what you have done. Guilt will eat away at you so much it will be difficult to function. Many people lose precious sleep over guilt; others can't eat – or eat too much – out of guilt. How do you respond to guilt? When you are burdened by guilt, you don't like yourself and you don't like anyone else because you are disgusted with you.

Guilt for most of us is like an old, familiar friend with whom we grew up. Most of us grew up being made to feel guilty about one thing or another. Most of us are living with wounds, with pain from our childhood, with some kind of guilt that was placed upon us. We learned to feel guilt and shame, often when we were too young to know what those emotions truly were. Those emotions followed us into adulthood. Contrary to popular belief, guilt is not normal, it's not natural. You have to learn to feel guilty. Guilt is not of God. Thank God that His forgiveness is not based on how we feel. Your forgiveness is in Christ Jesus. Therefore, if you are going to get to the point of really forgiving yourself, you must know your forgiveness is in the one who died for you, and you must focus on that rather than on your pain and "earning" forgiveness. You've got to stand on

Why Forgiveness Makes Sense

Romans 8:38 and 39, where Paul says he is persuaded that nothing can separate him from the love of God.

That means nothing. Not our guilt. Not our bad deeds. Not our angry words. And when we realize how fully God can forgive us, that gives us the framework for forgiving ourselves. We certainly can't refuse ourselves forgiveness when God so clearly shows an unforgiving spirit is not his spirit.

When you focus on God and His Word, it is only then that you can release yourself from the bondage of shame and guilt and receive grace. Forgiving yourself isn't about how much you do to "earn" your own forgiveness. It's about letting God shine through you, giving you the strength to forgive the person you had previously viewed with angry eyes.

Just one word of caution here. Many people will seek to remind you of your transgressions and will seek to stir up those old feelings of guilt. Do not let others determine whether you forgive yourself or not.

Outsiders never know your true state of mind or the totality of your experience. So they cannot be the ones to influence you to hold onto negative emotions that compromise your daily walk with God.

When someone seeks to bring up the negative things you've overcome and for which you've forgiven yourself, just politely cut them off. Tell them you've moved beyond that and do not need to repeat the experience. You've learned whatever lesson God had for you and you're allowing him to use that experience to do good.

Your spiritual walk is too important to allow in your path unnecessary roadblocks.

GREGORY KIRBY

"And be ye kind ... forgiving one another."

— Apostle Paul

Why Forgiveness Makes Sense

CHAPTER 8

Forgiving: The Steps

The previous chapters have detailed forgiveness and explained what it is and is not. You also now realize the importance forgiveness has in your daily life. So you are probably wondering, "OK, well, how do I forgive?"

It's easy to say, "We should forgive," but difficult to actually do. I've shared my own experiences and those of others I know to illustrate not only the transformative power of forgiveness, but also to give you hints on how to apply forgiveness.

Many will speak from the pulpit or from Bible classes and say forgiveness is simple. They will say that if you have Christ in your heart, forgiveness is instant. While this can be true, I think it is a bit naïve. We are at varying stages of Christian development, and it's unfair to make a new Christian, for example, think that he has somehow failed if he doesn't find forgiveness to be as easy as it has been portrayed to him.

Yes, ideally, we would all be mature enough as Christians and as individuals to never allow a slight to offend us and, if it does, to always readily and easily forgive. But that's not the world in which we live. We are human beings with complicated lives, faults, and needs.

Remember the story of Robert Newsome? He was a strong Christian by his own admission. But when he was shot and left for dead, it took him a while to allow forgiveness for his assailant and those involved to course through his being. Sure, someone could have preached damnation on Robert and could have beaten him down and told him what a bad Christian he was by not automatically forgiving someone who had tried to kill him, but where would that condemnation have lead?

A better way to address his lack of forgiveness would have been for someone to recognize that forgiveness isn't as easy as it sounds. That is the purpose of this book. I don't speak to you arrogantly, telling you your forgiveness should be instantaneous, instead of a spiritual journey.

The Lord recognized this, that is why there are so many scriptures about forgiveness in the Bible. He knew we needed constant reinforcement and we needed reminders and encouragement that forgiveness does come, no matter the hurt.

Unforgiveness is real. Just as hurt, hatred, and pain are real, unforgiveness is real. We certainly do not want to make light of your pain. In fact, sometimes hurt and pain are so bad until they seem endless. Sometimes we can hurt so badly, we wonder if the pain will ever leave. When you hurt like this, if you'll be honest, it seems a severe cloud of sadness has comes over your spirit. It seems you hurt so badly depression can set in, and you find it hard to move on.

The reason unforgiveness is so dangerous is when bitterness sets in, thoughts of seeking revenge occur. In as much as you want to get even, in as much as you want revenge, seeking revenge will only lead to more hurt and insult. Revenge will never satisfy as a repayment, retribution, or justice for the injury you have suffered. No repayment can erase what has been done to you. The only effective solution is to forgive the other person. Receive healing, and move on with your life.

By the very definition of forgiveness, it means to

Why Forgiveness Makes Sense

release the other person of their obligation, as we've learned. That's what messes us up. We feel that when we forgive someone and they are released from their obligation, we are letting somebody off the hook. We have a problem with that because we really want them to pay.

But I ask, why keep rehearsing your pain? Why keep reliving it day by day? Somebody did you wrong 20 years ago, yet it seems just like yesterday. Well, I wish I could tell you that if you keep rehearsing it, you could undo what has been done. But you can't undo it. No matter what the hurt, nothing that has been done to you is worth you having an unforgiving spirit. Nothing.

So then the question is, "How can I forgive and move on? What steps can I take?"

Jesus shares the keys to forgiveness in Matthew 5:43-44.

Steps to Forgiveness

"But I say unto you, love your enemies. Bless them that curse you. Do good to them that hate you. And pray for them which despitefully use you, and persecute you," says Matthew 5:44.

That's it in a nutshell. It seems simple, but we actually have a hard time with that.

That's why I will analyze this text here.

Love your enemies. Jesus says I know what you have heard, and I know what the common response to hurt is, but I say something different. Those who curse you and those who hate you, those who despitefully misuse you, those are the ones you should love. It can be tough to hear, that in spite of how someone abuses you, and in spite of how wicked and deceitful someone may be, Jesus says, "Love them." Jesus says, have compassion for them and good will toward those who wrong you. Love is the release valve that will set you free.

God is saying, "I am the answer." I know showing love like this is not what we expect today. Very few people show love in the age in which we live, so we think it an oddity. But my mama taught me to love. Folks sometimes look at me strangely when I show love or concern. That's because we see so often that when someone is "too nice," that means they are up to no good. So when we experience someone who is "too nice," and shows genuine Christian love, we don't know how to take it. We are suspicious of that love.

Once you could go to your neighbor for a cup of milk or a stick of butter and the neighbor was happy to give. Why? Because there was more genuine love. Whenever a person was blessed, she couldn't wait to share the blessing with another. Romans 5:10, says that God's love washed over us while we were yet dead because of sin. He loved us just the way we were. He expects for us to love one another.

Bless them that curse you. We must learn how to speak well of our enemies. Don't curse them back. Some of us come unglued and act like we are totally out of control when we are offended. We act like we lose our minds.

But that is not the model Jesus gives us. Conducting ourselves as Christians and showing love to one another is a matter of will and not of emotions. That's why the record says in Philippians 2:5: "Let this mind be in you, which was also in Christ Jesus."

In other words, it's a matter of the will. You can decide to exercise forgiveness. It's up to you.

When we respond negatively, while we can understand it because of our human tendencies, we must be

Why Forgiveness Makes Sense

honest with ourselves. Nobody can make us do anything. Nobody can make us become angry. Nobody can make us say and do insensitive things. It's up to us; we can decide if we're going to be kind or if we're going to act in a foolish way.

Romans 12:17, reiterates the point when it says don't go looking to repay evil with more evil. If somebody curses you, it will be evil to curse them back. First Peter 3:9 reinforces the call that we not become evil with those who become evil with us. You will be blessed when you conduct yourself in the Christian way of not repaying evil with evil.

Be a blessing, knowing this is what you should do so you may inherit good things. If you want to be blessed, learn to be kind. Many of us like to have the last word. I have a piece of advice concerning that as well: If you do get the last word – be sure it's a kind word.

Do good unto them. Not only should we learn to speak well and kind of one another, but we have got to learn to do well. If we are going to be on the road to recovery, then Jesus asks this of us. Jesus is not saying you are to be in denial about what someone did to you. He is not saying pretend it didn't happen or sweep it under the carpet. He is not even saying act like it's not a big deal. It is a big deal when somebody misuses you; it is a big deal when somebody mistreats you.

You know the Bible story of Joseph and how his brothers hurt him. We will explore it in more detail in another chapter, but Genesis 37 makes no secret of the fact that Joseph's brothers hated him and as a result, they betrayed him. Yes, that was a big deal. In chapter 50 of Genesis, when Joseph's brothers came to him in their time of need following their father's death, he didn't try to pretend that nothing happened. He said,

"Yeah, you hurt me, you were wrong. You meant me harm but God turned it into something good."

No, denial is not necessary. But, as we'll see later, Joseph didn't let his hurt keep him from doing a good thing. Joseph said, "I'm not going to try to play God and get even with you. I'm here to do whatever I can for you."

Romans 12:20 says if your enemy is hungry, feed him. If your enemy is thirsty, give him drink. Paul says for in so doing, you pile coals of fire on his head. Your kindness is a burning reminder that Jesus lives in you and that despite the evil that came from that person, you will not be swayed.

I have had some personal experiences with this particular step to forgiveness. I trusted a person and allowed him to get quite close to me, so close that I trusted this person with my business dealings. This person betrayed my trust, using the confidence I had placed in him as a means to manipulate me.

In essence, he stole from me, as his manipulation resulted in financial losses for me that threatened my career and even my family. He lied about the day-to-day operations of our joint ventures. As I found out about his duplicity, I was hurt and then angry and later, bitter.

I did not want to see this person; didn't wish him well. But after much prayer and conviction – because I knew better – the Holy Spirit moved on my heart. Oftentimes it's easy for us to say to other people to forgive when they have been violated, but when we have been stabbed in the back, we want to make exceptions to forgiveness. Well, I realized I was not above forgiveness and my case was not an exception. Forgiveness still had a place.

Why Forgiveness Makes Sense

I admit here that initially this situation was a real challenge to my faith, because the circumstance was so stressful and it took me quite a while to recover from the financial loss.

But I did recover. And I was able to do something good for this person. This man ended up having to come to me to ask for a favor, and I was willing to extend that favor. That's when I realized I had been able to work through and forgive this person. And now, he esteems me to others often. It's because of Christ in my heart that I have been able to reach out and do something good for the person who deceived and stole from me.

Pray for your enemy. This is serious. You must learn to pray for your enemy. Now, let me clarify. This is not about praying against the one who hurt, humiliated, or embarrassed you. Don't get on your knees and pray for God's wrath for your enemy. That's not it. This means pray for your enemy – in a good way. Do you seriously — on a regular basis — pray for somebody who has done you evil? That's just not something we tend to do. But Jesus says, talk to me about those who despitefully misuse you or who persecute you. Jesus says, "Just talk to me."

You don't have to fuss. Even if you feel you were unfairly treated and you are in a lose-lose situation, Jesus says pray about it. I know it's hard. Sometimes, your best intentions are met with negativity and you are hurt. Sometimes people do things to you on purpose. Sometimes it just seems that everyone else gets favor but you. But even in the midst of all that, Jesus says pray for your enemies.

In my life, I've been hurt the worst when I was only trying to help folk. It seems like I've been beaten up the worst when trying to be kind and to do good. Sometimes being kind can be risky business, but Jesus commands us to go forward in kindness and to pray to him and he'll ease our pain.

Now that I know Biblically based steps to forgiveness, I get great consolation when I pray. I can be sad when I know someone has despitefully misused me, but when I go down on my knees, I get great consolation just the same.

Jesus's simple clues are all the real and true steps we need to exhibit forgiveness. But sometimes we feel we need more help. Sometimes, because we are so hurt and angry, it's hard for us to clearly see how exercising what Jesus says in Matthew 5:44 can change our lives. It is for this reason that I am offering another approach to forgiveness. You may find after the exercise below, you have a clearer, more sincere mind to act on Matthew 5:44.

I know these steps work because they have helped me, as well as those I've had the opportunity to counsel.

How to Forgive

1. **Acknowledge the hurt.** Just as you did when you were doing the mental work that would prepare you to let go of the grudge, you must acknowledge that you are hurt. You must own what happened and how it affected you. Write it on a piece of paper, or share it with a trusted person who can encourage you.

2. **Examine yourself.** I know, when we are deeply hurt and angry, we don't want to look at ourselves. But we must be honest with ourselves, if we are to give forgiveness a chance. It's a lot easier to hold onto a grudge when we see ourselves as perfect victims. Perhaps we

Why Forgiveness Makes Sense

may not have been at fault in this particular instance, but have we ever done anything to hurt another? Have we ever lied or cheated or been rude or malicious? When we remember we are not perfect, we can be a little more open to the imperfections in others.

3. Check out the factors leading to hurt. Determine what exactly about this thing hurt you. Was it the act itself? Was it what you thought the act represented? Was it the words or the tone? Did you contribute to creating the situation in any way?

4. Pray for forgiveness. Ask God to forgive you for the negative thoughts you have had toward the person or people you are struggling to forgive. Ask God to heal your heart so you are open to moving forward, and not dwelling on the hurt.

5. Pray for the one who hurt you. That's right, pray for this person. Pray for the person you feel caused you this pain. In your prayer, say these words, "I forgive (name of the person) for (list the infraction)." Pray that God releases you from the bondage that has held you and that the person who hurts you gains God's forgiveness as well.

6. Pray with the person you have trusted. If you shared your experience with a trusted counselor or friend as discussed in the first step of this exercise, pray with this person. Each of you say a short prayer about this experience and your need for God's intervention.

7. Rip it from your life. Now, go back to the sheet of paper on which you wrote down the infraction you had to forgive. Look at it one more time. Hold the paper up and say aloud, "I forgive you." Rip up the paper and throw it away. If it is possible, practical, and can be safely done, consider having a conversation with the person you need to forgive. Let this person know you

have forgiven him or her, by God's grace. Speak in a tone that is not accusing, and use language that sincerely shares your forgiveness. It this is not practical, just stick to the paper ripping exercise.

8. Thank God. Thank God for granting you a forgiving spirit.

■

This exercise may seem complicated to you, but it doesn't have to be. Do not be so impatient that you skip a step. Each step is important. Each step has an emotional and a mental impact. If you skip a step, you short change yourself.

How do you feel following this exercise? Does your heart feel lighter? Do you feel at peace? Chances are, you do feel lighter. You may realize that full forgiveness has been granted on this day. If you are still struggling with forgiving what has happened, then pray on the matter for the next 21 days. Repeat the fourth step of this exercise, praying for the person and praying the prayer of forgiveness.

Consider as you go through this 21-day exercise how you can now apply Matthew 5:44 to this experience. How will you fulfill that scripture?

You will find that God does not lie. When we ask, we do receive. When you ask him to give you a forgiving spirit, he does.

Why Forgiveness Makes Sense

"Never does the human soul appear so strong as when it forgoes revenge, and dares forgive an injury."

— Edwin Chapin

GREGORY KIRBY

CHAPTER 9

Seeking Forgiveness

Sooner or later, every one of us needs forgiveness from another person, but many of us are reluctant to seek it – if we even admit we've done something wrong. We often try to justify our actions, to explain away our wrong or to make it seem like nothing.

It is important to recognize when we should seek forgiveness is important. From a Biblical standpoint, the Word tells us that if we have something against our brother, we should settle that before coming to the altar.

==Forgiveness cannot begin until we admit our own failure.== It cannot be initiated until we are willing to admit to ourselves that "I haven't really been all that." We must admit that we've not done all we could have and in some instances, we've even gone out of our way to do what we shouldn't have.

Pride often stands in the way of our admitting wrong doing. We want to pretend the offense never happened. I've witnessed some people try to evade their wrong doing by saying, "Let's just bury the hatchet."

That's the closest they get to even admitting they were wrong, all because they want to ignore what they did. But "burying the hatchet" doesn't work because that hatchet is still sharp, ready to be pulled out at the slightest provocation. We'd rather act tough and bad, still holding guilt and shame on the inside rather than admit our failure and show humility.

I know all of this to be true because I've been that person. I've already shared with you the pain of the unforgiving spirit I once harbored. There was a time in

Why Forgiveness Makes Sense

my life I would rather walk around and pretend to be tough than to admit that I had made mistakes. Some of us have a real problems being honorable enough to say, "I was wrong."

I know marriages right now that are on the rocks because of someone not willing to admit fault and say, "I really share some blame."

Five Steps to Seeking Forgiveness

There are five things we must do when we seek forgiveness. The reason I had for not acknowledging the wrong I had done to others was that I didn't want to deal with personal issues. The first issue we must deal with when we seek forgiveness is our own hurt.

Most of us will admit when we are mad, when we are glad, but it's another thing to admit we are hurting.

The second thing we must do is to choose to surrender totally to God's will. That means we must pray to God for forgiveness and seek his guidance, choosing to go according to his way, and not according to our own.

The third thing we must do when we seek forgiveness is to admit wrong doing. This one is the hardest for some people, as it requires that we bare all and accept responsibility. We admit that we were wrong, without rationalization; without making any excuses. Many of us will want to say something like, "I was wrong, but...." There is no "but." You were just wrong. It doesn't matter what another person does to you; that does not give you the license to blatantly do all manner of evil.

For example, if someone stepped on your toe and scuffed your new shoes, that doesn't give you the right to go off and curse that person out or to beat him up. Of course, the world would make allowances for things like that and will say that you have a right to get back at another, but we are not talking about the world. You don't have to follow everything everyone else does. You have a choice. I struggled in that area for a long time.

The fourth thing you must do when you are seeking forgiveness is to humble yourself to recognize and acknowledge the seriousness of what you have done. We've got to admit that when we hurt somebody, it is a serious offense. When we humble ourselves, we acknowledge our fallibility and our ability to cause pain.

The final thing we must do is take responsibility for restitution. We have a responsibility to not walk around talking about how time is going to heal the other person's wounds. Many of us take for granted that, if we just lay low long enough, the other person will be fine. We assume that if a span of time passes, all we have done will be forgotten and we hold no more responsibility.

That's not true.

Just because you haven't seen someone in five years doesn't mean all is well when you suddenly do see this person. If you have not tried to make restitution, then time has not just healed the situation. So part of seeking forgiveness isn't just about our prayer to God for it, but it is seeking the forgiveness of the person we have wronged, if at all possible, and trying to make it right.

Seeking forgiveness involves feeling true remorse for the wrong you have done. When you acknowledge what you did, without excuses, and seek to make restitution, this is a display of your remorse. You are sorry for what has happened. When we humble ourselves, we accomplish a lot more than if we stubbornly hold onto our haughty attitudes.

I worked with a couple who was having a hard time. The husband had done some things to hurt the wife

Why Forgiveness Makes Sense

deeply, and he was none too pleased with the wife. They wanted to save their marriage, but it seems they could not stop fighting long enough to do anything good for the relationship. By the time they came to me, they were visibly hostile, with each viewing the other as the enemy. Once they aired their hurt feelings and anger, I asked them each to see things from the other's point of view.

They realized they each had a part in the current state of the marriage. They each apologized to the other for the hurt and the pain. Those apologies opened the way for a whole new way of communicating. Once the wife got the apology she needed to be able to move on, and once the husband felt that the wife understood him, they were more open to each other.

Why did this happen? It happened because they were willing to humble themselves. ==Humility can open the door for a multitude== of opportunities.

When you get to the point of asking for someone's forgiveness, it doesn't have to be a complicated statement, but it does have to be sincere. Pulling together the steps we just discussed can come down to simply a few uttered words to the person you have offended. If a personal apology isn't possible or practical, a letter may be permissible. Craft your apology in the way that best conveys your remorse for what you have done and your earnest desire to make it right. If you are at a loss for words, here is a model to get you going.

Model for Seeking Forgiveness

Hi, (name of person), I am here to say I am truly sorry for the hurt I caused you. I am sorry for (name the thing). I will not do it again. Will you forgive me?

What to Do When Your Request Is Not Accepted

Sometimes, both the apology and plea for forgiveness are met with anger, disgust, indifference, or any number of other emotions. That can be disconcerting, especially if you've had to muster the courage to get the words out.

But do not let this discourage you. Your responsibility is to make the sincere effort to seek forgiveness. If the forgiveness is not granted, that is a matter the person must deal with between himself and God. You can't make someone forgive you, but you must do your best to make amends. If you have done your best with your sincere effort, then God recognizes this and your effort is sufficient.

■

Prayer to God for his forgiveness and the forgiveness of the one who has been hurt:
Dear Heavenly Father,
I thank you for the wonderful gift of forgiveness you have granted me in the Cross. I ask that you forgive me for (list the wrong.) I know it was not right and I am sorry. Please give me the change of heart not to do it again. Please also bless the person I've wronged so he/she forgives my action and has peace of heart. In Jesus's name, amen.

■

It Takes Strength to ask for Forgiveness

I struggled with asking people to give me something

Why Forgiveness Makes Sense

I had not been able to give, and that was forgiveness. I knew I had to change and let some stuff go and admit that I was holding onto both grudges and guilt. Our guilt is that shame we hold onto because of what we've done to others. We can't be healthy, happy, healed, and whole until we deal with guilt.

I've had some issues with some family members because of hurt. I left saying, "I don't care if I see him or her again. I've been hurt. Not only have I been hurt, but I've caused some hurt to family. Whether intentional or unintentional, the hurt is the same. I've had some issues I've had to settle myself, and I've even had some issues with God. When Mama went into the hospital for what was supposed to be a simple procedure and never came home, I had some issues with God. My mama was 62 years old, a woman who had tried to be faithful to God, and yet, suddenly, she was gone.

Yes, I had some issues with God. I couldn't understand why he let my mother die, and as a result, I held a grudge against my Heavenly Father. It's easy to blame others – even God – when we feel helpless in a situation. While there is no excuse for us to be angry with and resentful toward God, it is something a lot of people experience. But when we do experience that, we must find a way to break free from those irrational emotions. God is never the cause of our hurt.

In my experience, I finally allowed my faith in Jesus to help me to overcome this roadblock in my spiritual development. I thank God I've come to the point of my walk on this spiritual journey where I am more than convinced that forgiveness just makes sense.

GREGORY KIRBY

"Love me when I least deserve it, because that's when I really need it."

— Swedish proverb

CHAPTER 10

Forgiving When It Doesn't Make Sense

We can all understand if Robert Newsome had chosen not to forgive his attackers. After all, we generally think, all bets are off when it comes to someone trying to kill us. And we can all understand if someone who suffers an equally heinous crime chooses not to forgive, such as in the case of someone who has been a victim of rape or abuse.

We wouldn't blame them for being a little stingy in the forgiveness department.

There are just times when forgiveness doesn't make sense. Or it just doesn't make sense to our human understanding. Some sins are so egregious to us that a lack of forgiveness seems justified; even hatred seems justified.

This is where we are called upon as children of God to rise above even those very tough times. When it doesn't make sense to forgive, we can find the strength to do just that -- forgive.

I know at that particular time, it looks like a lost cause. Perhaps you've been in a dark place where it seems like every morning when you get up, your sunlight is eclipsed by dark clouds of sadness and despair. It's in times like these that we feel we are justified in holding onto our anger. It's in times like these that we feel that we have a right and a reason to hold a grudge based on the severity of our pain and the degree of our hurt.

GREGORY KIRBY

Just think about it. How can you let a person off the hook who has caused you so much hurt and so much misery? How can you forgive a person you've trusted when you find out this person has molested your daughter? How can you forgive a drunk driver who blindsides you while you are minding your own business, killing your three-year-old son? How can you ever forgive a trusted friend who assassinates your character and who spreads lies on you trying to ruin your credibility and reputation?

How can you let it go? When you know that you have been a good wife, doing everything a wife is expected to do, yet you discover that your husband has wrecked your home and run off with your best friend? How can you ever forgive?

The hurt is real, the pain is real. You live through the reality of being plagued by hurt, pain and frustration everyday. So oftentimes, we drown in our own sorrow. We become so caught up in what's going on with us until we are not sensitive to others who may hurt worse than we are. It seems there is no way out.

I've worked with people who have had these and similar experiences, and I'm sure you know of people who have been so hurt. Perhaps you are one of those people.

But the hope in this situation – and it may be hard for you to hear – is that it's not that you are unable to forgive. It's that you are unwilling to forgive. When you realize this, that gives your circumstance a whole new complexion. You have the ability. But do you have the inclination?

Remember our friend Robert Newsome? When he was shot with that long handled .38 caliber gun, he experienced hurt of a physical, mental, and emotional

Why Forgiveness Makes Sense

level. When he saw the man pull out that gun, he cried out, "Lord, help me."

When he was struck in the left leg with the first bullet, he cried out, "Lord, have mercy on me."

The second bullet struck him near the heart. Another bullet struck him in the arm, giving him an injury that remains to this day, as he is unable to lift his arm in a full range of motion. He later cried out, "Lord, save me."

Each of those pleas came back, fulfilled, though not in his time, but in God's. You see, even in our hardest times, we must invite God in to work a miracle in our lives.

Robert's life was spared that day as God answered his plea and saved him, but God also saved him, in due time, from a lifetime of bitter misery. Robert had to choose to be open to that forgiving spirit. When he became willing, he saw a change. It was then that he was able to forgive his assailant.

Let me tell you just to what extent Robert forgave.

He wrote a letter to the parole board on the gunman's behalf, sharing his forgiveness with those decision makers. Robert's words led to the gunman being released. But that wasn't the end of Robert's forgiveness. The gunman turned to him for a job. Robert, because he was now able to forgive, offered the man a job. (The man was unable to accept it, as the parole officer forbade the gunman to work for the man he had once shot.) The gunman asked Robert for money to help feed his family. Robert gave it to him.

Robert did not just speak forgiveness, he lived it, even if it seems to us that forgiveness in that instance didn't make sense.

The gunman went by Robert's office one day and

said he was sorry. Robert said, "It's OK, brother. I forgive you."

Robert embraced the man who had once tried to kill him. He let his life be a testimony to that man on that day. Robert said, "I want you to know I love you, and I want to help you."

Robert has told me and he has told my congregation that it took a power greater than he, to forgive his assailant. "Without God fixing it up for me, I couldn't have done that."

When we are open to God fixing it up for us, it can happen. Sometimes it's about doggedly focusing on his word, despite our natural inclinations to do otherwise. Other times, it is through a constant state of prayer that we experience a change of heart.

I have a Biblical example for you as well. We mentioned it in an earlier chapter, so let's explore it in detail here. In the story of Joseph and his brothers, in Genesis 37, we see a bit of family strife. Somebody can identify with drama at home. Perhaps you are going through a situation within your own family where you're not getting along, or someone downright does not like – perhaps even hates – you. So was the case with Joseph.

He had been violated badly. He was disappointed by people he trusted. You know what it's like when you have been hurt by people you trust. In Joseph's case, he shared a dream he had and his brothers couldn't cover their resentment of him anymore. He was already their father's favorite, and this dream, which portrayed Joseph as a leader among his brothers, was too much. In a fit of jealousy, they threw Joseph in a pit.

Sometimes, you have to make a decision in the pit. The pit is a metaphor for the low place in which you find yourself. What decision will you make while at

Why Forgiveness Makes Sense

your low point? Joseph made a decision to build on his relationship with God while he was in the pit. He realized you can't depend on anyone but God when you are in the pit. Joseph handled his situation while he was yet in the pit. When it looked like there was no hope, he relied upon God.

It's in the pit that we confront our own truths and make immediate decisions of whether we will hold on or let go. We have to decide right in the pit whether we will trust God or whether we will take matters into our own hands.

Sometimes, even as we make a decision to stay focused on God and to work through our issues, it seems that things go from bad to worse. In Joseph's case, he was sold into slavery. Imagine. First your brothers double cross you and leave you in a pit in the middle of nowhere, then you are sold into bondage: all because your siblings were jealous!

Anger and bitterness could have easily poisoned Joseph. Some of us are living with betrayals. We've been living with them for one, two, five, ten, 20 years, and if we are to be honest, we are in the pit. We can't get out of the dumps because we will not allow our hearts to soften. When people hurt you, the after effects can be repeated troubles in your life.

Joseph experienced such troubles. After being sold into slavery, he eventually was cast into prison, after refusing to commit adultery with a man's wife.

Yet, in the midst of trouble, he stayed focused on God. Sometimes when you are going through, it looks like God has forgotten all about you, just as it may have appeared the case for Joseph. But after 13 years, word reached the king that there was a man in prison who can interpret dreams. It was because of this that Jo-

GREGORY KIRBY

seph found favor with the king.

I believe God allowed Joseph's trials to be a part of his triumph, giving us a reminder that even our toughest hurts can have a good outcome – if we keep our minds on good and not on evil.

Joseph went on to become second in command, an elevated leader in the land. When a famine descended upon the area, Joseph's brothers ended up coming to him for food. It turned out Joseph was able to help his family and save his countrymen from starvation.

This started out of something bad – a family betrayal. But it ended in something good -- his being in a position to help those who sought to do him wrong. If you stay attuned to God and don't try to take matters into your own hands, God has a way of leveling the playing field.

Joseph was in a powerful position and he could have sought revenge on his brothers. In fact, his brothers were fearful of this very thing when their father died. They thought, surely Joseph would take the opportunity to get back at them.

But Joseph's forgiveness was complete. He wept at the idea that his brothers thought he had not forgiven them. He recognized he could not be their judge and told them all was forgiven between them and him. "I am not God," he said. He said that they meant all that had happened for evil, but God meant it for good.

When our hearts are so broken by hurt and it seems unreasonable to forgive, we must remember these stories. We must remember Robert Newsome, who forgave and helped a man who shot him four times. We must remember Joseph, who suffered years of pain because of family jealousy. Yet both of these men found it in their hearts to forgive. Their path to forgiveness was

Why Forgiveness Makes Sense

in God.

And did you notice one other thing about each of their paths to forgiveness? Each of them helped those who hurt them. Yes, that's right, they worked their forgiveness. Robert helped to free the man who gunned him down, and even gave the man money. Joseph gave his brothers food and support to take them through the lean years.

If you let God settle the score, God will work it for your good.

Our human understanding tries to make us think we have a right to hold onto bitterness and unforgiveness because we want to see the person who hurt us suffer and hurt the way we hurt, but we can't be free like that. Satan will tell us it doesn't make sense to let this person off the hook; God's Word tells us it doesn't make sense to keep yourself in bondage.

Check out this modern-day illustration of a person refusing to be in bondage. This example happened many years ago when I worked in corporate America. There were two coworkers who had some personal issues with each other. Both of these were professing Christians, but their actions left much to be desired. One of the individuals schemed to get the other fired. He succeeded.

The guy who was fired knew his adversary had a hand in the firing. Predictably, the job loss caused an even bigger rift between the two, as the one who was now without employment experienced a financial hardship because of the setback. Suddenly, his family was facing financial ruin, and he blamed the other man.

He scrambled to find a new opportunity as a means to support his family. The man who was fired could have held onto his initial anger and resentment, and most people would have expected it. After all, if we feel someone else caused us to lose our job, many of us would be quite hostile. But this man didn't dwell in the pits of feeling sorry for himself. Instead, he moved on with his life. He ended up in a much better position, running his own business. He made a lot more money, had more time to devote to his family and his church, and found an all-around better quality of life.

That is not where the story ends. The man who was fired went back and apologized to the other man, repenting for his part in the strife between the two. He even went on to be a financial blessing to his former coworker and enemy.

The lesson from this is that even in the midst of hardship, we have to be open to what God can do through seemingly total disaster and hardship. We have to keep our Christian perspective and not become vengeful. What if this guy had done something to hurt the other man? What if he had retaliated and done something with far-reaching and negative consequences? Instead, he was able to turn around and forgive the man who caused him so much harm.

No offense is too great that we can't move beyond it.

The Road to Forgiving the Seemingly Unforgivable

The reasons for this forgiveness are the same as we've discussed: forgiveness is about healing ourselves. If we hold onto the seemingly justified emotions toward someone who has committed a serious offense against us, then we allow that person and those actions to hurt us over and over again. We then are unable to move

Why Forgiveness Makes Sense

toward healing.

Sometimes professional care helps. If you have suffered such a circumstance, perhaps counseling with your spiritual leader, your pastor, or a licensed therapist would be beneficial. Do not be ashamed if you need outside help. Sometimes, people outside a particular situation can help shed light that you may be unable to see because you are involved. When I am counseling with those who visit with me, for example, I often try to bring up points they may not have considered, and often, those discussions can be turning points.

When it doesn't make sense to forgive, God gives us special scriptures to help us through. I know it seems unfair, but God doesn't tell us it's OK not to forgive if someone slaps us, versus if the person pinches us. He doesn't tell us it's OK not to forgive if someone lies on us versus if the person laughs at us. He doesn't make a distinction between offenses.

When it doesn't make sense to forgive, and we are able to, then that is when we can see evidence of Jesus in our lives. It's at those times that we realize we are growing in faith and in execution of that faith.

While there are times when hurt seems to last for a while before it dulls, there are many instances in life that, because of Jesus, we are able to experience instant relief. That is the encouragement I share with you today. Even if you've suffered great hurt and you can't see how you can ever forgive the offender, I tell you that it is possible.

Our continued communion with God allows us to transcend common emotions. That's not to say we won't be hurt, but it is to say we will have a strong spiritual foundation whereby we are able to judge our hurts. If we do not have a connection with God, it is easy for us to feel hopeless and helpless, and to succumb to our human thoughts that some things can't be forgotten. But if we are working on our relationships with God on a regular basis through prayer, meditation, Bible study and fellowship with other believers, we are feeding our spirits a diet rich in God's love.

This is ultimately what helped Robert Newsome forgive those who sought to take his life. He renewed his connection with God. Sometimes our connection with God is strained, especially when we are not seeking to know him on a personal level. When that happens, our emotional states go into decline.

Depression, low self-esteem, and even poor personal perception are all the result of an imbalance in our lives. Many life coaches, speakers, and authors focus on the psychological components of these mental and emotional issues, but we as Christians must also realize there is a spiritual component. One who is out of fellowship with God will feel at a loss. Many people who are out of fellowship with God experience mental turmoil, but they don't know why. They attribute it to all manner of other things, except their spiritual lives.

When we have strong spiritual lives (and we can all stand to grow in this area), we realize things we had originally thought impossible now are very much possible.

Ways to Strengthen Your Connection With God

1. Begin each day with sincere prayer. Go before God each morning, talking with him, and listening to him. Pray about your concerns, your goals, your wishes. And listen to what he is telling you. Pour out your heart to

Why Forgiveness Makes Sense

him, but also pray that you grow in understanding of his will for your life and that your heart grows more like his with each day.

==2. Study his word.== God has revealed his nature to us through the Bible. Take time each day to let him speak to you as you study your Bible and reflect on what is in its pages.

==3. Commune with others.== Fellowship on a regular basis with other believers so that you are encouraged and can learn as you study and worship together.

Do not mope if you do not have a strong connection with God right now. That is why you are reading this book -- to learn. You can start today to work on your relationship with him. That way, whether you are struggling now with a forgiveness issue, or you may one day face one, you can be prepared.

Yes, forgiveness is possible, even when it doesn't make sense.

GREGORY KIRBY

"**Forgiveness is the fragrance of the violet which still clings fast to the heel that crushed it.**"

— George Roemisch

Why Forgiveness Makes Sense

CHAPTER 11

Reconciling and Trusting After Forgiving

When someone has been hurt by actions of another, either because of intentional injury, willful disregard or even malice, she may wonder just how far she must go in forgiving. "Must I reconcile with the person once I've forgiven him?"

The answer is, not necessarily.

I addressed this a bit in a previous chapter, but I will elaborate here. God doesn't require that we become buddy buddy with someone who has callously hurt us. Sometimes, it's not wise. Other times, it's not even possible.

But as much as it is feasible, it is his desire that we make things right between ourselves and others. "If it be possible, as much as lieth in you, live peaceably with all men," Paul says in Romans 12:18.

Paul acknowledges that sometimes, it's not practical for us to get along like best friends. So he said, "If it is possible…"

Even when it is not possible to resume or have a relationship with the person you have forgiven, you do your best to live in peace, without strife. You show mercy to that person and no longer have a desire for revenge.

What About Trust?

Remember earlier when we said to experience true forgiveness, we must also forget? Well, forgetting has two meanings. It is true that we must forget in order to forgive. We cannot hold onto the negative emotions and keep throwing those at the one we claim to forgive. And so in that sense, we must forget.

But forgetting on an emotional level does not mean forgetting on an intellectual level.

What do I mean? What I mean is that we base trust on our experience and knowledge of that person and tendencies; that requires learning lessons from those experiences.

Trusting Is Not the Same As Forgiving

It is possible to forgive a person, but not to trust that person. That is because forgiveness means, as we've learned, a release from the resentment and anger toward a person. Forgiveness is about letting go of the grudge.

Forgiveness is a heart issue, but trust must be a head issue. If a person has been repeatedly untrustworthy, God doesn't expect you to go back to trusting that person. It is foolish to ignore reason and sound judgment. Your decisions must be made from a vantage point of intelligence and critical thinking. If he has revealed to you the true nature of that person and your experience tells you this person makes decisions that are not in your best interest, then to trust that person would not only be foolish, but potentially unsafe.

There are times when a situation may allow trust to be restored. I've counseled couples who have faced issues of broken trust. Some of those couples are able to regain trust after they have discovered and faced the problems and fixed the root causes.

Why Forgiveness Makes Sense

The partner who has forgiven recognizes that the partner who broke the trust will not do those same things again, and therefore trust can be rebuilt. In those instances, an honest approach to the problem opened the way for renewed trust.

GREGORY KIRBY

"Lord, make me an instrument of thy peace. Where there is hatred, let me sow love. Where there is injury, pardon."

— St. Francis of Assisi

Why Forgiveness Makes Sense

CHAPTER 12

Inviting A Life of Abundance

When we release ourselves from the strongholds of an unforgiving spirit, we open ourselves up to so much. We open ourselves up to abundance, because we are no longer being stingy in our love. Do you not know that forgiveness is a reflection of love, don't you?

God wants us to have an abundant life. Please understand, he doesn't mean for us all to become millionaires overnight or never have to lift a finger to work. That is the world's view of abundance. God wants us to have abundance in so many areas – he wants us to have rich relationships, full lives, etc. He wants us to have abundance in our personal, spiritual, and career lives. If that results in a healthy balance sheet, that's great. But that's not all there is.

We invite a life of abundance when we finally get it about forgiveness. The previous chapters are designed to help you finally get it. This chapter is about helping you rebuild your life after you've become free.

What do you crave? Do you crave healthy relationships? Do you crave wellness of body and spirit? Do you crave a solid career? All of this can be yours, now that you no longer are in the grips of bitterness and anger.

The power of life is in the tongue. When you speak evil of or to someone, you are speaking evil to your own self. Think about that for a moment. All those times you said terrible things about the person who hurt you, you were hurting yourself. All those times you went out of your way to harm the one who hurt you, you were harming yourself. All the times you allowed darkness to take control of you, you were moving further away from God's light of abundance.

Jeremiah 29:11 tells us that God wants abundance for us. Are you ready to seek it in your life?

If you are, then you must take an active role in creating that abundance. Often, some will teach that we have no control over our lives, or that we are just victims of our own selves. That is not the true Christian's view. We know that the opposite is true. God gave us all free will. He gave us the ability to make choices that can enhance our lives, or harm our lives. When we think of our lives from a spiritually empowered position, we then realize just how much stake we do have in our earthly lives, even as we are assured of a heavenly life.

Have you behaved in a spiritually empowered way or a spiritually imprisoned way? If you have been spiritually empowered, then you have actively worked to make choices that move you further toward your goals. If you have been spiritually imprisoned, then you have been content to let others make choices for you.

I want to encourage you to live in a spiritually empowered way.

When I began to live in a spiritually empowered way, I noticed immediate changes. For one, I was more joyful. I could view the world as full of promise instead of full of hurt. I could open myself to see the other abundance God had for me because I had changed my focus. I was no longer devoting so much time to hurt.

My relationships improved and so did my ministry. I've since become a sought after presenter who spends quite a bit of time on the road, sharing information with others. I've been able to plant churches and see them grow, and even write and publish books. All of

Why Forgiveness Makes Sense

this abundance could not have been possible if I continued to live in spiritual imprisonment.

What abundance have you held back in your life because of spiritual imprisonment? Are you stuck in your career or unable to get it to the next level? Can your marriage or friendship be restored if spiritual imprisonment is replaced with spiritual empowerment?

I will go back to Robert Newsome's story. When he released himself from the spiritual imprisonment he had boxed himself into, he found restoration. His wife, who had left him in the midst of the chaos, returned home and they've grown closer and stronger in the years since. He has been blessed to share his story before audiences, including my congregation. He has gone on to face and win against other challenges.

Yes, I know it is possible to find abundance after spiritual imprisonment.

GREGORY KIRBY

"There is no remedy for love but to love more."

— Henry David Thoreau

Why Forgiveness Makes Sense

CHAPTER 13

Rebuilding Life After a Broken Trust

Rebuilding life after a betrayal is not easy. But you can grow from your experience and move forward. This book is about healing your heart and rebuilding your life. While we've spent much of the time up to now focused on healing the heart through forgiveness, we cannot forget that there is more to the equation.

The other part of that equation is figuring out how to regain your life. We will address both rebuilding your life if you are the one who broke trust and sought forgiveness as well as rebuilding your life if you are the one who granted forgiveness to someone who broke your trust.

In the chapter on reconciling and trust, we realized it is not necessary to trust a person after he has betrayed that trust. We must evaluate each situation and judge it on its own merits. Some circumstances allow trust to return; others do not.

But we must remember trust is a complicated matter. Trust is based on an expectation that the person is someone we can rely on for whatever the reason we grant the trust.

Restoring Trust After Someone Has Betrayed You

If we want to trust the person again, our expectations must be met. Rebuilding trust with someone who

GREGORY KIRBY

has lost face with you involves a process. What is the process? The person must satisfy in you the question you have concerning whether he or she is trustworthy. The person can do this through a series of words and actions. A person just declaring that he can be trusted won't get far after he has blown that trust. Instead, he must assure you that the situation of the broken trust will not come again. This is often done by explaining why the trust was broken and sharing how the situation has been addressed so it will not be repeated. But because we have an innate self-protective desire, we are not easily convinced. So the assurances often must be repeated. But not just in words.

More important to the process of rebuilding the relationship and trust is in the offender's actions. We must see through the actions that this person has changed and that this person will not again let us down. When we are assured through the combination of words and deeds that this person again can be trusted, only then are we able to reconnect with that person on a level of trust as we seek to regain ground in the relationship. As we discussed earlier in this book, the relationship may not be the same. But it can be redeemed – if, and only if – our trust is regained.

But what happens when we are the ones who broke trust and who are seeking the forgiveness? There will no doubt come a time in your life when you will do something to hurt another – perhaps it's a spouse, maybe it's a friend, possibly it's a child. Whoever it is your actions hurt, you may have a deep desire to rebuild your life following the damage your actions caused. Part of rebuilding your life may mean getting back in the good graces of the person you offended.

If that is the case, then you'll have some homework

Why Forgiveness Makes Sense

to do. We assume you've already sought forgiveness from the person with whom you wish to restore relations. Well, seeking forgiveness is only the first step to rebuilding the relationship and your life.

Here are some other keys.

Keys to Fostering Trust After You Have Let Someone Down

1. Share what you feel. Express to the person what the loss of the relationship has meant to you. Let the person know you understand that you have done wrong and you are here to make it up. Ask the person if he or she feels you two can regain what was lost and possibly move on to something even better.

2. Ask for a roadmap. Ask the person with whom you would like to restore relations what it is you can do to make the situation right. Be open to the suggestions if they are reasonable.

3. Realize rebuilding doesn't happen overnight. Know that while the person may have forgiven you, she may need some time to see what you truly are about. Know that she may need to see that you can be trusted again, not just hear it. Which leads us to our fourth point:

4. Show integrity. Clearly demonstrate that you are an upstanding person who acts with integrity. Make sure what you say matches what you do. If you say you will be at an appointment at 5 o'clock, be there at 5 o'clock. It may seem like a small thing, but it's not. Every action you do will either contribute to your case for regaining trust, or it will work against it. By doing something as "small" as maintaining a schedule, you show that you are conscientious and live by your word.

5. Be caring. Show the person that you care about

him or her and that you will not do anything to harm.

6. Be sincere. The worst thing you can do when you are attempting to rebuild a relationship and regain trust is to come off as "fake." When you engage in actions with the goal of rebuilding trust, make sure you are doing things that are in keeping with your character and that you are operating out of a real desire to do better. If you come across as not meaning what you say or what you do, then your quest to regain trust and rebuild the relationship will be lost.

Realize You Have the Power to Make Good Choices

Sometimes as you struggle to put your life back together, you face very real concerns: how can I ever regain the smile I had before this betrayal? What happens if I forgive this person and let him back in and am hurt again?

Well, I'm sorry to say, there are no assurances that you will never again be hurt. But you can still rebuild your life. The key to regaining your smile or determining whom you will trust is in realizing that you are in control.

Yes, you. When we feel at others' mercy, then we feel like victims. That's when we are fearful of trusting because we have handed over our power. But when we realize we can decide who gets our trust and to what degree we will put ourselves at risk of hurt, then we are free to trust. It's when we feel we are surrendering ourselves and have no control that we feel we are vulnerable.

When you are struggling to overcome a hurt and rebuild your life, honestly examine what you want from

Why Forgiveness Makes Sense

the situation. Then figure out how you will get there. Do you truly want to restore a relationship with this particular person, or are you open to new experiences with others? Do you want to regain a lost situation, or are you now ready to embark on something new? How has this experience changed you and how can your new circumstance meet the needs of the person you have become?

Choose A Positive Course of Action

Choose to think about your experience in a positive way. Now granted, no betrayal or hurt feels good, but life does not bring us through an experience for naught. No matter what trial we endure, God leaves at least a nugget of a blessing. I have seen people who have weathered unimaginable pain emerge from their experiences to do good work. Some have realized they could be embittered by their experiences or they could search for the blessing, and so they chose to search for the blessing. A parent who lost a child to a drunk driver may have started a scholarship fund for other children. A woman who was betrayed by her spouse may have formed a support group to help others. A home owner whose house was burglarized may have decided to start a community safety program.

Often when we choose to do something good, we recover more quickly. Even if we don't feel very cheerful at the outset, we can look up and realize that our choice to be proactive actually does lift our spirits. No, our doing good work does not erase the bad thing that happened, but it can sure give it a different perspective.

Rebuilding your life is about your choice to emerge

from your experience as a victor and not a victim. When you realize this, then you are able to move beyond the thing that happened to you and allow God to work through you.

Why Forgiveness Makes Sense

"A wise man will make haste to forgive, because he knows the true value of time, and will not suffer it to pass away in unnecessary pain."

— Samuel Johnson

GREGORY KIRBY

CHAPTER 14

Exercising Forgiveness, Now and Forever

The lessons you've learned in this book are aimed at helping you create forgiveness in your life, both by your extending forgiveness to others and receiving it as well. You've received motivation as well as Biblical evidence to help you on your journey.

Your charge now is to manifest this forgiveness in your life and to create a continuous fountain of love by sharing what you have learned with others. You no doubt can identify others who may be struggling with a lack of forgiveness. How can what you have learned here be applied to their experiences?

Perhaps you will be able to share what you now know with someone. If you see someone who can benefit from the lessons of forgiveness, approach him with a genuine spirit of love. Consider that the person already is hurting, so how you approach him is critical. Do not go to the person with a judgmental or hostile tone. Pray before you approach the person who has your attention.

As for the right words and the right tone of your approach, consider them of utmost importance. Sometimes, the reception we receive isn't about our words, but about how we organize those words and how we say those words. Your goal here is not to further hurt someone by coming across as holier-than-thou or as insensitive. None of us can judge another's soul.

When you approach the person, begin by sharing

Why Forgiveness Makes Sense

why you have come to this person. Let him or her know you are there because you care. The person may bristle or become offended, but that's all right. Speak calmly and be open. Invite the person to pray with you and to share what she is feeling. Often, a friend is all that is needed for a person to open up.

If the person chooses to share her emotions with you, know this is very personal. Do not make derogatory comments, even if the person expresses bitterness or anger. At this point in the conversation, when you are inviting the person to confide and share with you, you are here to be of comfort.

After you have allowed the person the opportunity to express his emotions, look to God for guidance. He will give you the best way to proceed. Again, be mindful of your tone and your words.

Use scripture to support what you are telling this person. Explain why forgiveness is important and what it means. This isn't about what you think or your emotions, it's about helping this person learn that forgiveness can be attained and it's required.

Just as I know it is my duty to help others after God freed me from the grips of bitterness and anger when I was able to forgive, it is your duty as well. Go forward and spread forgiveness.

Go spread love.

GREGORY KIRBY

"Forgiveness is the final form of love."

— Reinhold Niebuhr

Why Forgiveness Makes Sense

SCRIPTURES ON FORGIVENESS

We must always be prepared to make our points with sound Biblical references. Below are some key scriptures used in this text that point to the importance and practice of forgiveness. Consider the scriptures on their own as well as the context in which they are used. The Bible is full of scriptures in both the Old and New Testaments that point to forgiveness and love.

Romans 12:2

Key point — *Renew your mind.* Change your mind and how you view your trials, hurts, and needs.

First John 1:9

Key point — *Confess sin and God will forgive.* We must acknowledge our wrong and seek forgiveness and it will be granted.

Mark 11:25:

Key point — *Forgive others so God will forgive you.* We can't hold unto unforgiving spirits, yet expect God's forgiveness.

Matt 18: 21-22:

Key point — *Forgive as much as necessary.* Our forgiveness should know no bounds.

Luke 23:34:

Key point — *Jesus asked for the forgiveness of those who killed him.* Jesus shows us there is no hurt too big that we can't forgive.

Matthew 18:21-35

Key point — *Parable of unforgiving servant.* How can we refuse to forgive something small when God forgives us of the largest infraction?

Why Forgiveness Makes Sense

Romans 12:17

Key point — *Do not get stuck doing bad things to those who do bad things to you.*

Romans 12:18

Key point — *Live peaceably.* As much as is in your control, be at peace with those around you.

Isaiah 53:5

Key point — *Jesus was wounded for our wrong.* Jesus has already paid the price for whatever wrong we have done and will do.

First John 2:1

Key point — *Jesus is the advocate.* Jesus intercedes on our behalf.

Romans 8:38-39

Key point — *Nothing can separate us from*

God's love. We should not be afraid that our wrong wipes away God's love for us.

Matthew 6:9-13

Key point — *The Lord's Prayer.* Jesus's short model prayer includes forgiveness.

Matthew 5:43-44

Key point — *Love your enemies.* Behave in a loving spirit toward those who hurt you. This is the crux of what it means to forgive.

Romans 12:20

Key point — *Serve your enemy.* Feed him. Clothe him.

Philippians 2:15

Key point — *Have a mind like Christ.*

Jeremiah 29:11

Key point — *God wants good for us.* God

Why Forgiveness Makes Sense

wants abundance for us.

First Peter 3:9

Key point — *Again, no evil for evil.* It doesn't matter what the wrong done to you is, your response must not be wrong in return.

GREGORY KIRBY

Gregory Kirby is a pastor, presenter, and author. He travels the nation conducting training sessions, workshops, and seminars on a variety of ministry-related topics. Pastor Kirby is an expert on matters of church growth — including church planting, ministry organization, and leadership development.

He is a graduate of Louisiana Tech University, with a Bachelor of Arts degree in Speech Communication. He also studied at the University of Arkansas and Southwestern Theological Seminary in Fort Worth, Texas and received a Master of Divinity in Church Growth and Evangelism.

Kirby is founder of Nationwide Christian Ministry Fellowship, which provides a nurturing environment for those in ministry. The organization provides resources, training, and networking opportunities. He also is the Pastor of Steeple Chase Baptist Church in Shreveport, La.

Gregory Kirby also is the author of *Giving an Invitation for a Positive Response: Closing the Deal on a Divine Destiny.*

Why Forgiveness Makes Sense

Learn from Gregory Kirby himself!

Get ready for exciting, up-beat, educational training

Ready to take your spiritual walk to a new level? Let Pastor Gregory Kirby help you. Pastor Kirby is a skilled and expert presenter, as he breaks down complicated matters into understandable, relevant pieces. Whether you need him to present a church growth talk at your next conference or need him to conduct a leadership training retreat for your staff, he can meet the need. And while he spends much of his time conducting events related to these matters, he also works with individuals, groups, and organizations on topics pertaining to personal growth, including forgiveness, goal attainment, and relationship management.

He creates customized programs designed for each particular audience.

Call (318) 686-8600 to book Pastor Gregory Kirby for your next event.

GREGORY KIRBY

Grab a book full of tips
to enhance your ministry

Are you a pastor or preacher looking for new ways to share God's love? Well, pick up a copy of Pastor Gregory Kirby's *Giving an Invitation for a Positive Response: Closing the Deal on a Divine Destiny.* This book includes innovative tools, tips, and strategies to take your invitational appeal to a higher level.

Order your copy at www.gkirby.org or call (318) 686-8600. Or Write to Gregory Kirby Ministries, P. O. Box 19003, Shreveport, LA 71149.

Why Forgiveness Makes Sense